Castles and Cathedrals

STUART FRASER

Hodder & Stoughton

LONDON SYDNEY AUCKLAND

ACKNOWLEDGEMENTS

The Publishers would like to thank the following for their permission to reproduce illustrations: La Bibliotheque Nationale, Paris cover; p37. Michael Holford p4; p7; p8 left. English Heritage p5 top; p18; p22 left; p25; p28; p56; p58 both; p61 top. The British Library p8 right; p20 both; p24 left; p30 both; p57 left. The Fitzwilliam Museum p9. By permission of the Syndics, Cambridge University Library p11 left. A.F. Kersting p11 right; p16 top. John Bethell p12 left; p62 left. Reproduced with the permission of Shropshire County Council p12 right; p14 top. Aerofilms p13; p15; p38 lower. Reader's Digest Association Ltd p14 lower. By permission of The Master and Fellows of Corpus Christi College, Cambridge p16 lower; p45. Woodmansterne p17; p23 left. Hever Castle Ltd p22 right. Jerry Sampson p24 right. English Life Publications Ltd, Derby p27 both. Derek A Edwards/Norfolk Landscape Archaeology Section of the Norfolk Museums Service p32. Bodleian Library, University of Oxford p34 left; p43; p46. Archbishop of Canterbury/The Trustees of Lambeth Palace Library p34 right. By permission of The Master and Fellows of Trinity College, Cambridge p35. Wales Tourist Board p36 right; p38 top. La Bibliotheque Municipal, Dijon p40 both. National Library of Air Photography/Royal Commission on the Historical Monuments of England p41. The Mansell Collection p44 left; p54. Sonia Halliday p48. The National Portrait Gallery, London p55. © The National Trust 1992 p57 right; p62 right; p63. Leeds Castle Enterprises Ltd p59. Education Officer, Shropshire County Council p60 left. Winchester Cathedral p60 right.

The cover illustration, from a French 14th-century manuscript, shows the siege of Jerusalem, 1099.

British Library Cataloguing in Publication Data

Fraser, Stuart
   Castles and cathedrals. – (Past historic)
   I. Title   II. Series
   ISBN 0 340 55066X

First published 1992

© 1992 Stuart Fraser

Illustrations by Joseph McEwan

All rights reserved. No part of this publication may be reproduced or transmitted in any form or by any means, electronic or mechanical, including photocopy, recording, or any information storage and retrieval system, without permission in writing from the publisher or under licence from the Copyright Licensing Agency Limited. Further details of such licences (for reprographic reproduction) may be obtained from the Copyright Licensing Agency Limited, of 90 Tottenham Court Road, London W1P 9HE.

Typeset by Litho Link Ltd, Welshpool, Powys, Wales
Printed in Great Britain for the educational publishing division of Hodder & Stoughton Ltd, Mill Road, Dunton Green, Sevenoaks, Kent by Scotprint Ltd, Musselburgh

CONTENTS

1	The Norman Conquest – Castles	4
2	The Norman Conquest – Cathedrals	8
3	Castles as Centres of Power	12
4	Cathedrals as Centres of Power	16
5	Castles as Places to Defend	20
6	Cathedrals as Places to Impress	24
7	Life in the Castle	28
8	Life in the Abbey	32
9	The Castles of Edward I	36
10	The Monks of Fountains Abbey	40
11	Nuns	42
12	Friars	44
13	Chivalry	46
14	Heraldry	50
15	Tournaments	52
16	The End of the Monasteries	54
17	The End of the Castles	56
18	Fieldwork – Castles	58
19	Fieldwork – Cathedrals and Monasteries	60
20	Change and Continuity	62
	Glossary	64
	Index	65

The further we go back in time, the more we have to depend upon buildings to provide the clues to people's activities.
Alec Clifton-Taylor, 1975.

THE NORMAN CONQUEST – CASTLES

| 1000 | 1100 | 1200 | 1300 | 1400 | 1500 |

1066 is probably the most famous date in English history. It was the year of the Battle of Hastings and the beginning of the Norman Conquest. The man who became the first Norman king of England is known as William the Conqueror. William had to do more than win one battle to take over England. He had to increase his power until he could claim the whole country as his own.

William was able to take and hold onto the country by building castles. This stopped the defeated English from rebelling against their new rulers. The first castle was built at Hastings soon after William set foot on English soil. This castle is shown on the Bayeux Tapestry, which tells the story of the Norman Conquest.

A The Normans building the castle at Hastings.

The first of these forts were built in a hurry and followed a simple basic plan. They were called motte and bailey castles. The motte was a steep mound of hard-packed earth, flattened on the top. The earth for the mound came from a circular trench dug around its base. This ditch became part of the defence.

The level top of the motte was surrounded by a stockade of sharpened stakes, and some form of wooden tower would be put up inside. A wooden bridge over the ditch joined the motte to the bailey. This was an enclosure surrounded by an earth bank with a wooden parapet on top and a ditch in front.

We know what they looked like because some people who saw these castles wrote about them.

B A Norman called John of Colmieu was one. He wrote about them in about 1130:
It is the custom of the nobles of the neighbourhood to make a mound of earth as high as they can and then encircle it with a ditch as wide and deep as possible. They enclose the space on top of the mound with a palisade of very strong logs firmly fixed together. Within the enclosure is a house, a central keep which commands the whole of the surrounding wall.

Usually the wooden keep was small. It must have been very cramped to live in. Sometimes, though, the keeps were fairly large.

C One of these was described by Lambert of Ardes in the 12th century:
The first storey was on the ground level, where there were cellars and grain stores and great boxes, barrels, casks, and other household objects. In the storey above were the dwelling and common rooms of the residents, including the larders, pantry and kitchen and the great chamber in which the lord and lady slept. In the upper storey of the house were attic rooms.

> Historians base their accounts of the past on what has survived. When very little has survived it may not give us a very good idea of what the normal castle was like.

1. Written descriptions of motte and bailey castles are rare. Why must we be careful when we are using these descriptions to find out about them?
2. Why does source A not tell us much about what motte and bailey castles looked like?
3. a) Apart from written sources and pictures, what else can we use?
   b) Why may these not give us a complete description of motte and bailey castles?

As peaceful times became more frequent, many of the smaller castles were gradually abandoned. The bigger castles were repaired when their wooden defences began to rot and decay. Now the barons could afford to take their time and use stone to replace the wood. The wooden tower on top of the motte was replaced by a strong stone keep. The wooden stakes around the bailey were replaced by a stone wall.

D A modern artist's impression of Portchester Castle in Hampshire.

In many of the royal castles the keep was a large building with several floors. In the smaller castles the keep was probably only used in an emergency. The daily life of the castle must have carried on in the bailey. This would have been filled with buildings such as a kitchen, a chapel, and a stable, as well as sleeping quarters for the soldiers.

> History is about things changing over time. To see how things change we need to compare things by looking for similarities and differences.

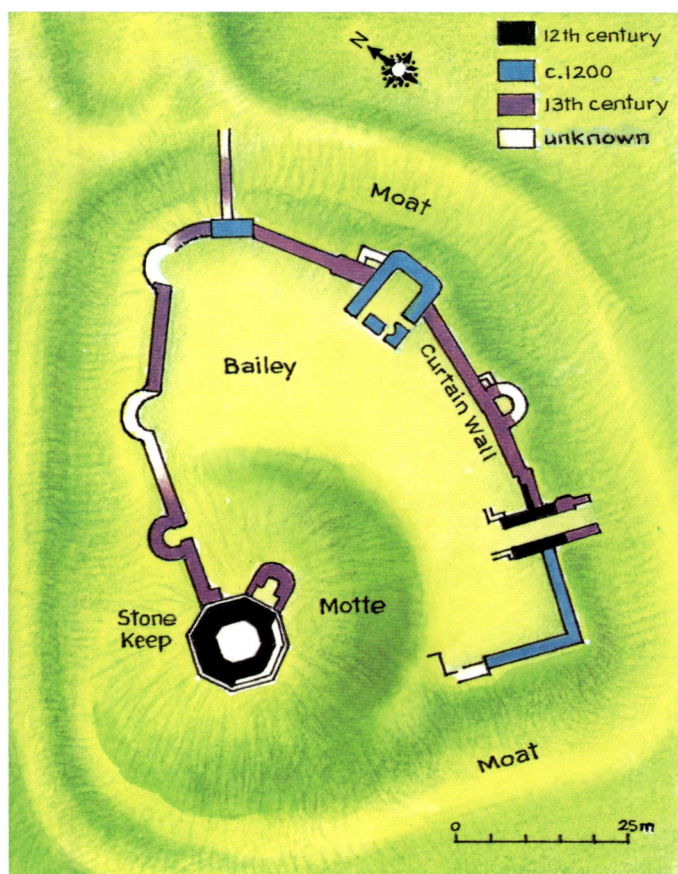

E Plan of Richard's Castle in Shropshire.

4 Explain the similarities and differences between the castles in sources A and B and source D.

5 Explain the similarities and differences between the castles in sources A and B and source E.

6 a) What is missing from source E?
   b) Draw the plan and add the missing parts showing clearly what they are.
   c) Suggest a reason why the person who drew source E was not able to show the missing parts.

BARONS AND CASTLES

When William became the king of England the whole country was his own property. However, he could not control all the land himself. So he gave lands to the men who had fought for him at the Battle of Hastings. These men became the leading barons who ruled parts of England for William.

A William of Poitiers said what happened in *History of William the Conqueror* (1074).
> He placed capable leaders with ample forces of knights and foot soldiers in his castles, men brought over from France whom he could trust and knew were able.

As the Normans conquered more and more parts of England, so more and more castles were built. By 1087, 50 castles were recorded in the Domesday Book. The castles had to be put up quickly. The early motte and bailey castles used only materials that were available nearby – earth and timber.

Safe within their castles, the Norman barons could keep the English under control. The castles showed that the Normans intended to hold onto what they had conquered. The castles were resented by the English people.

B This is what a motte and bailey castle might have looked like.

C Cross-section of a motte and bailey castle.

D The *Anglo-Saxon Chronicle* tells us how they felt:

They [the Normans] built castles far and wide throughout the land, distressing the wretched people, and thereafter, things went from bad to worse.

E According to the *Anglo-Saxon Chronicle* things did get worse. One of the last entries has this to say:

1137 Every powerful man built his castles . . . and they filled the country full of castles. When the castles were built, they filled them with devils and wicked men. Then, both by night and day, they took those people that they thought had any goods and tortured them with horrible tortures to get their gold and silver.

They were hung by the thumbs or by the head, and heavy armour was hung on their feet. Knotted ropes were put round their heads and twisted until they went into the brains. They put them in prisons where there were adders and snakes and toads, and killed them like that.

Castles served as a base from which the barons would raid the surrounding area with an armed force to put down rebellions. They also served as a place of safety in times of danger, when the castle had to be defended against an attacking force.

F A castle being set on fire – a picture from the Bayeux Tapestry.

To understand history we need to ask why things happened. We often find that there is more than one reason.

1. What caused the Normans to build motte and bailey castles?
   Here are some possible reasons:
   (i) The materials – earth and timber – were easily available.
   (ii) They were quick and easy to build.
   (iii) They were easy to defend.
   (iv) They were a way of showing the power of the barons.
   (v) They provided homes for the barons.
   a) Rewrite the list putting the most important reason at the top, with the least important at the bottom.
   b) Explain why you chose the order you did.
   c) You may add any other reasons you can think of.

History is about results as well as reasons. When things happen you often find that there are several results.

2. What were the results of the barons building castles?
   Here are some possible results:
   (i) The barons were able to keep the country under control.
   (ii) They caused resentment and anger amongst the English.
   (iii) They gave the barons a place of safety in times of danger.
   (iv) They gave the barons a place to keep a small army of knights and soldiers.
   a) Rewrite the list putting the most important result at the top, with the least important at the bottom.
   b) Explain why you chose the order you did.
   c) You may add any other results you can think of.
3. As a group, compare your answers. Can you agree on the main reason and result?

2 THE NORMAN CONQUEST – CATHEDRALS

1000   1100   1200   1300   1400   1500

When King William gave land to Norman barons throughout England, he also put Norman bishops and abbots in all the most important posts in the Church. The barons had castles to show how powerful they were. The bishops had cathedrals.

The bishops were usually too busy to spend much time in their cathedrals. The king would often expect the more powerful bishops to help him rule the country. When William the Conqueror took over England he relied on his bishops as much as his barons to help him. His own brother, Odo, was a bishop. He made his friend, Lanfranc, the new Archbishop of Canterbury. When William was out of the country for any reason Lanfranc would rule England for him.

Odo was Bishop of Bayeux in Normandy. It was he who had the famous Bayeux Tapestry made. He took part in the Battle of Hastings.

B A Bishop from a medieval manuscript of the 13th century.

A Bishop Odo during the Battle of Hastings, from the Bayeux Tapestry. He is shown wielding a mace and encouraging Norman warriors to carry on fighting. He is not wearing full armour. This suggests he did not actually fight and shed blood.

We look at the evidence to find out about the past. For example, what sort of men were the bishops? Sometimes the evidence does not agree. Historians have to compare sources in order to reach conclusions.

1. Compare source A and source B. What different impression do they give of bishops?
2. What can we learn about the job of a bishop from sources A and B?

Just as the barons had to provide knights to serve the king, so the bishops and abbots had to do the same.

C *The Abingdon Chronicle* (c.1150) explained:

Castles were raised at Wallingford, Oxford and Windsor, and at many other places, for the defence of the kingdom. The abbey was ordered by royal command to have a guard of knights at that same Windsor Castle.

The king did not expect the abbot and his monks to fight. Instead, they rented out land to knights who in return provided the service that the king demanded. The abbey was able to do this because it owned a great deal of land. Some of this was granted by the king, but much of it was given by barons. They thought they were buying a place in heaven. If they did not go to heaven they believed they would end up in hell.

D A 14th-century painting by a monk called William de Brailes shows the horrors of hell.

> 3 Why did the monks make pictures like source D?
> 4 What did the monks hope people would think when they looked at the picture?
> 5 How do we know that people believed the pictures were true?
> 6 Why do we find it difficult to take pictures like source D seriously?

In 1067 William the Conqueror founded Battle Abbey on the very site of the Battle of Hastings. William gave land and money for the abbey as a thanks offering for beating King Harold's army. He insisted that the altar should be built on the actual spot where Harold was killed.

DURHAM CATHEDRAL

Another way in which a church might become wealthy was by attracting pilgrims. One of the finest examples of an early Norman Cathedral is Durham. This became famous because it held the body of Saint Cuthbert. Although St Cuthbert had been dead for hundreds of years, the monks behaved as if he were still alive.

In 1160 one of the bishops began to add a new chapel to the east end of the cathedral. They had not got far when cracks began to appear in the walls. The monks thought this was a sign that St Cuthbert did not want a chapel built so close to his shrine. So the monks promptly gave up and began again at the west end.

Durham became a great centre of pilgrimage. Every pilgrim was expected to bring a gift to the shrine of St Cuthbert, so the cathedral collected a great fortune. This made it possible for the bishop to build a new cathedral in the latest style.

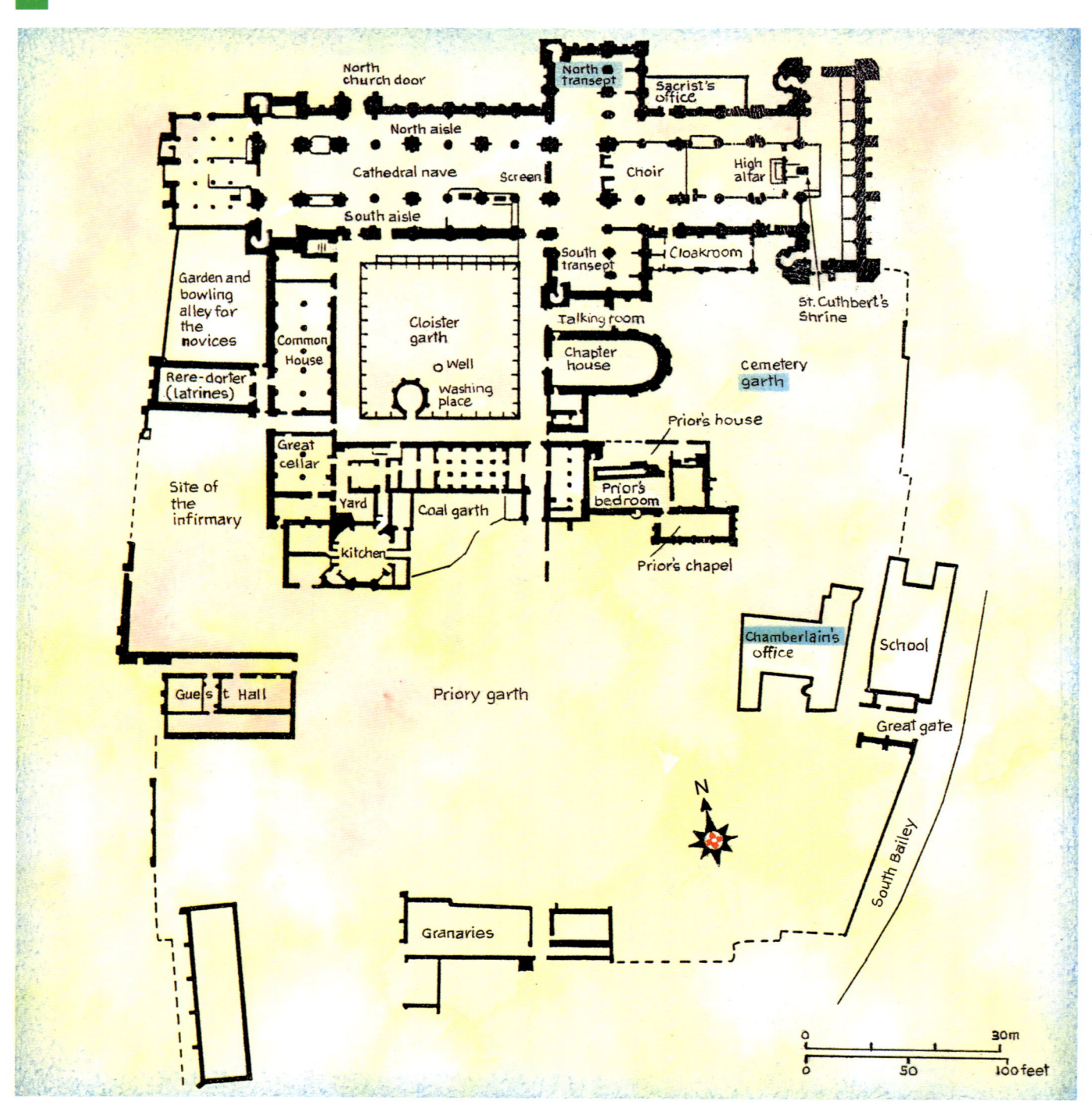

A Plan of Durham Cathedral.

B This description of St Cuthbert's shrine was written in 1593 in the *Rites of Durham* by an old man who had been a monk of Durham in his youth:

The shrine was decorated with most elaborate workmanship of fine and costly green marble all lined and gilded with gold. It had four seats or places under the shrine for the pilgrims or lame men sitting on their knees to lean and rest on. The shrine was so richly decorated that it was said to be one of the most expensive monuments in all England.

C A 14th-century picture of pilgrims at a shrine. One of them is kneeling partly inside the shrine.

As well as crowds of ordinary pilgrims, kings and rich barons visited the shrine. By giving gifts to the church they hoped it would be easier to go to heaven.

Men might approach the saint's shrine, but women were never allowed to do so. There was a line of black marble stretching across the floor at one end of the cathedral nave. Women were not allowed to go beyond this.

In 1333 Queen Philippa happened to be staying in Durham with her husband, Edward III. She was occupying a room in the prior's lodgings. To her surprise she was awoken in the middle of the night and told of the saint's dislike for women.

The queen got up, and, dressed only in her nightclothes and a cloak, went out through the great gate of the monastery. Although it was a chilly night, she went past the east end of the cathedral and along Dun Cow Lane to the castle. It would have been quicker, and not so cold, to go through the cathedral. Why did Philippa not go this way?

D The nave of Durham Cathedral.

People living at the time would not have been surprised by Philippa's actions. They would expect Philippa to obey the rule which said women must not go near the shrine of St Cuthbert. Nowadays we are surprised at Philippa's behaviour. We might think she was superstitious, afraid of the dead or just ignorant. She certainly seems to have accepted that women must obey the rule. We live at a different time and have different ideas.

> When we learn about people in history we need to understand why they behaved as they did. We need to look at things through their eyes.

1. How would one of the monks living at Durham explain Philippa's behaviour?
2. How might we explain Philippa's actions today?
3. Why did the king not try to stop Philippa going to the castle?
4. Why did the monks look after St Cuthbert's shrine very carefully?
5. What did pilgrims expect to gain by visiting St Cuthbert's shrine?

11

3 CASTLES AS CENTRES OF POWER

1000　　　1100　　　1200　　　1300　　　1400　　　1500

CASTLES OF THE WELSH MARCHES

When the Normans came to England they had to take over the country by force. William the Conqueror and later Norman kings relied on the barons to keep the defeated English under control. Castles were built to show that the Normans were in command – and had come to stay. Each castle dominated the surrounding countryside and made clear who was in charge.

Many castles were built in areas where there was danger of rebellion. One such area was the borderland between England and Wales, known as the Welsh Marches. Several uprisings in this area led to the building of castles to watch over the Welsh.

It was important that a castle was carefully sited if it was going to command the surrounding area. There were several things that a baron might look for when choosing a suitable place to build a castle. These included:
- high ground overlooking the surrounding countryside.
- a gap in a range of hills.
- a river with bends in its course.
- being close to main overland routes.
- where a river crossing was provided by a bridge or ford.

Ludlow Castle occupies one of the best sites in the Welsh Marches. Roger de Lacy built it in 1085. The river protects it on three sides. On the north and west approaches there is a steep cliff face almost 30 metres (100 ft) high. The stone for the building of the castle came from the rock on which it stands.

Roger de Lacy understood the advantages of Ludlow as a site. The importance of Ludlow Castle gave rise to a new town. This was built on the gentle slopes between the castle gate and the banks of the River Teme where it is crossed by Ludford Bridge.

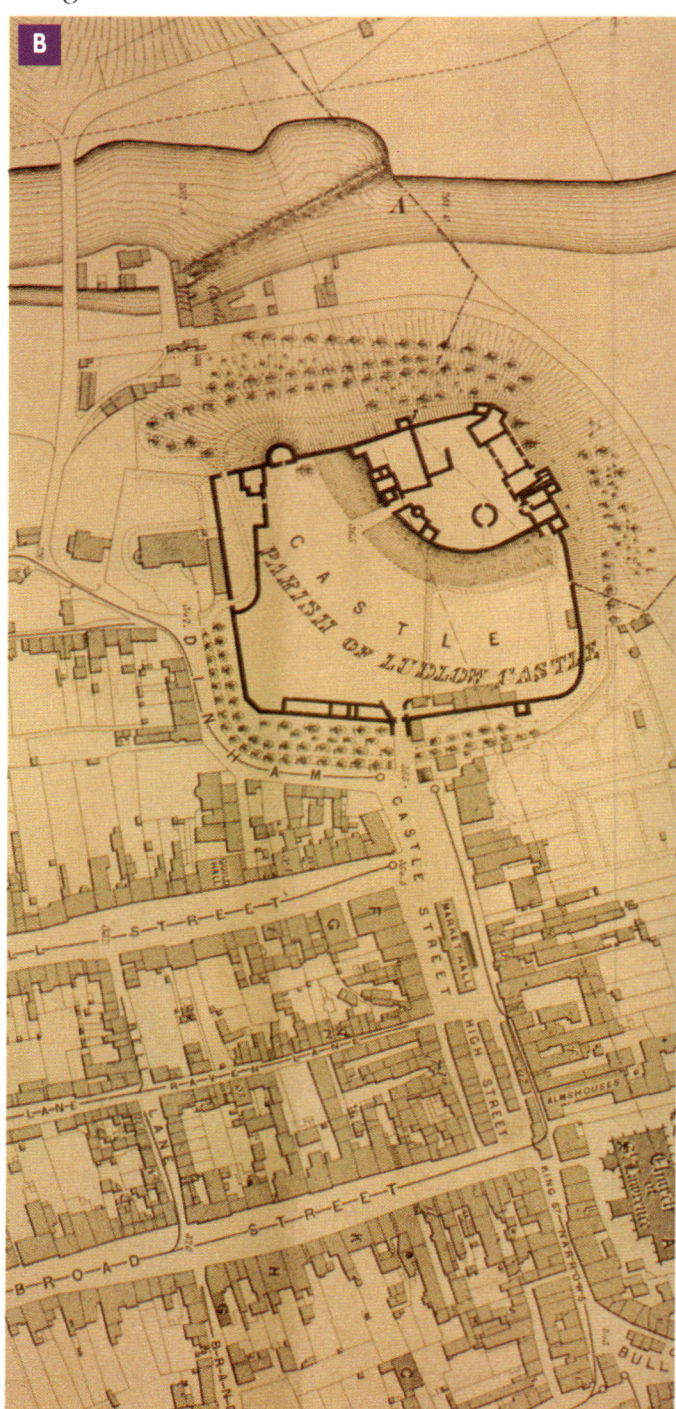

Baron Roger knew what he was looking for when he chose Ludlow as a place to build a castle. There are several sources available to help us understand why Baron Roger chose Ludlow.

A variety of sources can be used to get the information we need to understand the past. For instance, we can use photographs and plans.

1. Which of the three sources (A, B or C) is:
   a) a plan of Ludlow?
   b) an aerial photograph?
   c) a photograph taken from the ground?
2. a) Which of the five features that made a site suitable did Ludlow Castle have? Explain how you decided.
   b) What other advantages did the site of Ludlow Castle have? Explain your answer.
3. Using source C, from which direction would the defenders of the castle expect an attack? Give reasons for your answer.
4. From which direction is source A looking? How did you work out your answer?
5. Using sources A, B and C, what obstacles would attackers from that direction have to overcome?

SHREWSBURY CASTLE

Another example of a castle in the Welsh Marches is Shrewsbury. There are many different sources about the site of Shrewsbury Castle. Sources A to C are examples.

Before the Normans came Shrewsbury was called Scrobb's-burg, meaning Scrobb's fortified place. It lies in the centre of Shropshire, on high ground in a loop of the River Severn. The castle had an oval motte with an inner and an outer bailey. In 1069 the castle was attacked unsuccessfully by the Welsh.

A Old map of Shrewsbury.

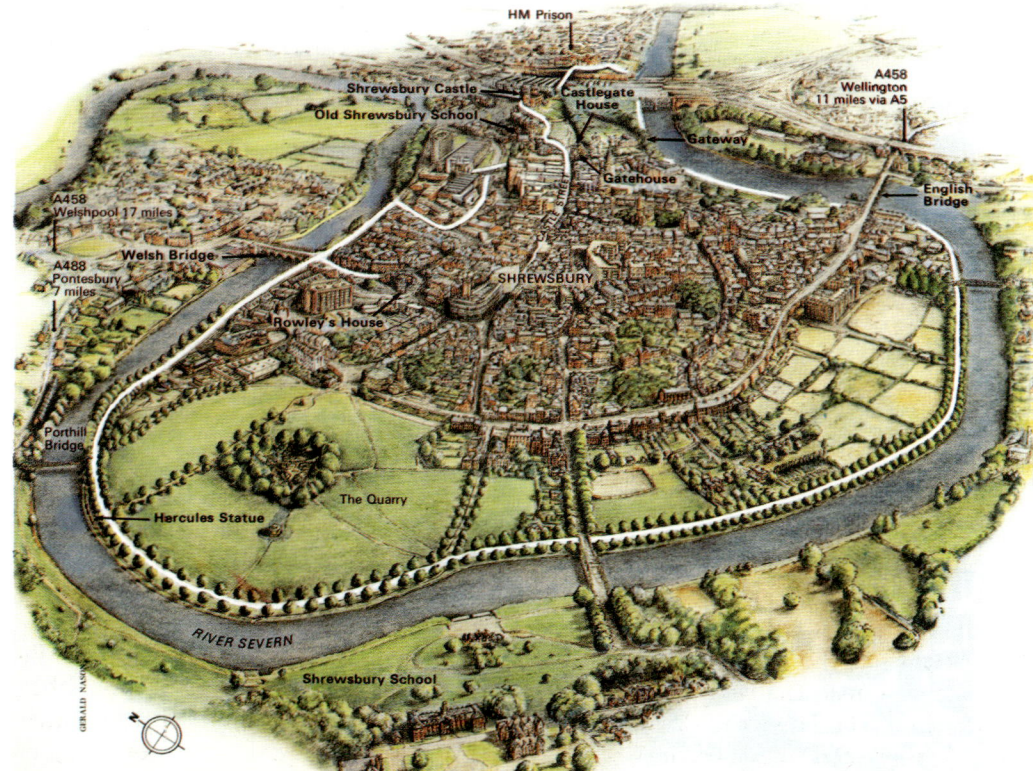

B Modern map of Shrewsbury.

14

C Aerial photograph of Shrewsbury.

> When we use sources to find out about the past we need to know how useful they are. Some sources have more value than others.

1. What are the advantages of using an old map?
2. What are the disadvantages of using a map like source B?
3. What are the advantages and disadvantages of A and C compared with B?

The castle was built by Roger of Montgomery soon after the Norman Conquest. He was one of the chief barons who came over with William the Conqueror. The Domesday Book records that 51 houses were destroyed to make way for his castle.

D A book called *The History and Antiquities of Shrewsbury* written by T. Phillips in 1779 has this to say about Roger:

The Earls of Shrewsbury kept their court there, this being the capital of the earldom; they had lower barons under them, who met to discuss all important business . . . These barons probably were such as held land of the Earls' in Shropshire. Roger of Montgomery had almost the whole of the county given him by the king, to whom he was closely related.

In medieval times there were two bridges crossing the River Severn at Shrewsbury. They were called the English Bridge and the Welsh Bridge. Today the names survive but the old bridges have been replaced by new ones.

4. a) Using sources A, B and C draw a sketch plan of Shrewsbury (only showing the main features).
   b) What big advantage did Shrewsbury have as a site?
5. Mark on the plan where you think Roger would have built his castle. If you look carefully you might even be able to spot it. Source B will help you.
6. From what the Domesday Book says, how was Shrewsbury different to Ludlow?
7. a) How do you think the two medieval bridges of Shrewsbury got their names?
   b) Using source A as evidence, explain how the Welsh and English Bridges were defended.
8. Why was William prepared to give Roger control over such a large area?

Apart from the castle, the largest building in medieval Shrewsbury was the abbey. In many ways the two buildings were rivals. Both the baron in the castle and the abbot in the abbey tried to increase their power over Shrewsbury and the area around it. We have seen that castles were centres of power. The same was true of abbeys and cathedrals.

4 CATHEDRALS AS CENTRES OF POWER

A Tithe barn for storing produce from the monastery's farms. Its size shows how much land the Church owned.

If you went back to the middle ages many things would seem very different. The towns would be much smaller and most of the buildings would be made of wood and thatch. There is one type of building, however, that you would recognise. A lot of them are still around today because they were made of stone. Virtually every town and village had one – it was a church.

Churches were built of stone because they were the most important building in the town or village. They were also the biggest buildings. But most churches were small compared to the great cathedrals and abbeys. The size of these showed everybody how powerful the Church was. No expense was spared to make the cathedrals and abbeys as impressive as possible.

The power of the Church, though, was nothing to do with the fact that it owned a lot of large buildings. The Church owned something far more valuable – land. Apart from the king, the cathedrals and abbeys were the biggest landowners in the country. Many people depended on the Church for a living, since almost everybody worked on the land. Either they would rent land from the church, or they would farm the land for the Church.

As the cathedrals and abbeys owned so much land, the bishops and abbots had to be good businessmen. They had to run their estates efficiently in order to make money. The church estates would be divided into manors or individual farms. Some of the farms were called granges and were usually farmed by the monks themselves. Other farms and manors were let to tenants who paid their rent in corn and other goods.

Another way of getting money was from a special tax called the tithe. This was a tenth of the food produced by a farmer. This produce was given to the local church. Some abbeys owned parish churches and so they took the tithe. There were even monasteries that owned mines and some that ran markets in towns.

B A dispute over tithes. The monk is pointing at the writing on the page. This is to remind the peasants what they owed the church.

C Salisbury Cathedral. This would cost millions of pounds to build today.

Some monasteries owned whole towns. The town of Battle had grown up at the abbey gates, on the abbey lands. Other towns had been given to the local monastery by the king. The people who lived in the towns did not always like having the monks in charge. They complained about the money they had to give to the abbey or cathedral.

In Shrewsbury there was a longstanding dispute between the abbey and the leaders of the townspeople, called burgesses. When Earl Roger founded the abbey he gave it three mills. Henry I gave the abbey the sole right to grind corn in Shrewsbury.

This was very profitable for the abbey since it meant that the townspeople had no choice. They had to use the abbey's mills and pay what the monks demanded for it.

D The Cartulary of Shrewsbury Abbey recorded this in 1121:
> Henry, King of England, informs Robert, bishop of Coventry, and Richard, bishop of London, that he has granted the whole multure of Shrewsbury to the abbey. No mill or fishery is to be made at either bridge or in any part of the city.

As Shrewsbury grew in importance the burgesses tried to break this law. During the Barons' War of 1264–6 the burgesses put up mills without permission. They thought they might get away with it because they supported the king. Henry would help them for being on his side.

The abbey supported the rebel baron Simon de Montfort. It was out of favour with the king. The result was an agreement allowing the town to keep some of the mills it had put up.

E This is how it is recorded in the Cartulary of Shrewsbury Abbey:
> An agreement made before the king and his council at Shrewsbury on Friday, 23 September 1267, between the burgesses and the abbey concerning the erection of mills against the privileges of the abbey. These are three horse-mills and one windmill in the town and three horse-mills in the suburbs. Three horse-mills are to be destroyed but the four mills inside the town walls shall remain.

The story did not finish there since the abbey complained that it was losing money. The monks blamed this on the burgesses, amongst others.

F In 1312 the abbey complained to the Bishop of Lichfield about the problem:
> The abbey's possessions outside Shropshire are mostly in the Marches of Wales, and they have been plundered, burned and stolen by the Welsh. Moreover the marcher barons have taken the abbey's land and reaped the profits. Their mills have lost money by the violence and greed of the burgesses of Shrewsbury and their property in the town destroyed by fire.

1. Why was it important for the abbey to stay on good terms with the king?
2. Why do you think the abbey supported Simon de Montfort?
3. a) What reward did the town gain by supporting the king in his struggle with the barons?
   b) How did the power of the abbey suffer as a result of supporting the wrong side?
4. What were the burgesses being accused of doing in source F?

In 1381, the people of some monastic towns joined in the Peasants' Revolt. The townspeople demanded freedom from the power of the monasteries. At Bury St Edmunds, peasants and townsmen executed Sir John Cavendish, the king's chief justice. They then advanced upon the abbey carrying his head on a pike.

The prior fled, but was found hiding in a wood near Newmarket. After a mock trial he was beheaded. At the abbey itself another monk was killed. About £1,000 worth of treasure was seized by the rebels, and much damage was done.

5. Which sources show that people did not accept the power of the Church without questions? Explain how you decided.
6. What complaints do you think the peasants and people of Bury St Edmunds had against the abbey?
7. Explain the link between:
   source A, source B and source C.

HAUGHMOND ABBEY

Haughmond Abbey in Shropshire was founded in 1135 by Augustinian monks. It was surrounded by woodland. As soon as the site of the abbey was chosen, the trees were cut down to make way for the buildings. The monks also began the work of clearing land around the monastery to turn the woodland into fields for farming. Keeping sheep could be very profitable. The abbey was only four miles from Shrewsbury, which was a centre of the wool trade in the 13th and 14th centuries.

The land on which the abbey was built was given by William Fitzalan, who was a wealthy baron. Gradually the abbot and his monks added to the land owned by the monastery. The abbey continued to receive gifts of land from people wanting to support the work of the monks.

Sometimes the monks were given large estates by wealthy landowners; at other times they would receive small amounts of land from farmers and traders. Eventually the abbey owned land all over Shropshire, as well as in neighbouring counties. This property brought much money to the abbey either through the sale of farm produce or through the rents from tenants.

A The ruins of Haughmond Abbey today.

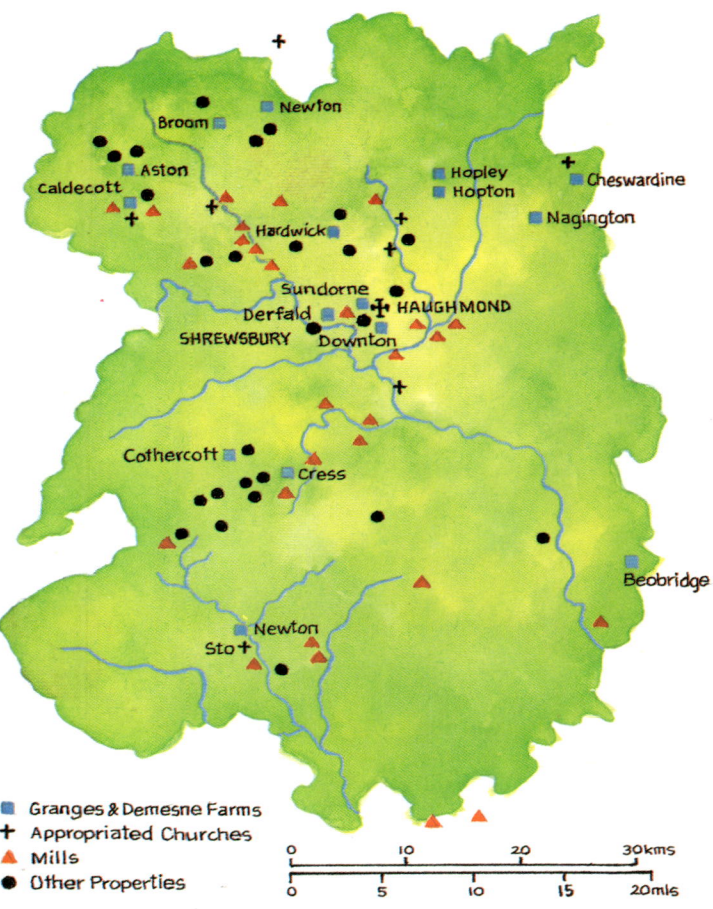

D This agreement is about renting two of these shops:

> Agreement between the abbot and convent on the one side and Philip Corbet and Alice his first wife on the other whereby the abbot and convent lease to Philip and Alice for their lives two shops in Shrewsbury market... The tenants are to pay 19s [95p] annually at the gate of Haughmond for the support of the poor and 5s [25p] to the infirmary on the feast of St. John the Baptist.

This shows how the monks spent some of the money they received. Sometimes the monks held services for the people who gave them money. A popular example of this was paying for the monks to pray for your soul after you died. The idea was that when you died your soul would go to a place called purgatory.

There you were punished for all the bad things you had done in life. It lasted until all the evil was got rid of by fire. This was very painful. If the monks prayed for your soul its passage through purgatory would be quicker.

E This is an example:

> Thomson son of Robert Maudut confirms the gift of Robert his grandfather and Agnes his mother. One monk is to pray for his soul and those of his ancestors.

The monks also made money from people who paid to be buried in the abbey. This was quite an honour – but it was expensive. Rich tenants could pay for the privilege with a suitable gift.

B Map showing land owned by Haughmond Abbey. A demesne was land owned by the abbey. Appropriated churches were under the control of the abbey. This meant that they had the right to the tithes.

The abbey owned several other types of property apart from land. The monks owned mills in various parts of Shropshire. Some of these mills were fulling mills which cleaned and thickened woollen cloth. The abbey also owned barns which it rented out.

C This is an example of an agreement about renting a barn:

> Alan Taplin acknowledges that he owes 6d [2.5p] a year for his barn in Coleham between Alan Poer's barn and Roger Feirwin's. He has [not made] this payment but has been convicted of this before the church court. Therefore, by this charter, he confirms the rent and promises that, if he or his heirs fail to pay within eight days of the feast of St. Michael, they must pay double.

As you can see the monks were hard-headed businessmen! They were also involved in property development. They bought land in the old market of Shrewsbury in order to put up shops and create a medieval shopping centre.

When we want to find out about the past we need to look at several sources. Each source can add to our knowledge. For example, sources C, D and E are written sources about Haughmond Abbey.

1. a) Which sources mention what the money received was used for?
   b) What were these uses?
2. a) Which source mentions a penalty for not paying on time?
   b) What is the penalty?
3. Which source shows that people thought that the soul's journey through purgatory would be a long one? Explain your answer.
4. a) What effect do you think owning so much land had on the religious work of the monks in the abbey church?
   b) Why do you think some monks had to spend time away from the abbey?

5 CASTLES AS PLACES TO DEFEND

A Women attacking a castle from a 13th-century manuscript.

ATTACK

Against the castle every means of attack could be used. The attacker had four basic options:
- to go over the wall
- to go through the wall
- to go under the wall
- to starve out the defenders after a long siege.

A scaling ladder could be used to get over the wall. This would be difficult since the wall might be as much as ten metres high. Also, to get to the foot of the wall there was usually a moat to cross. A large number of ladders would be needed to enable enough men to attack at the same time. Before this could be done the moat would have to be filled in some way.

A siege tower was another way of getting in. This was a tower made of wooden scaffolding. It had wheels so that it could be pushed into position. When a drawbridge was lowered from the top of the tower, the attackers would rush over onto the wall of the castle.

B Scaling ladders being used.

the old tower. A mangonel on the south and one on the north made two breaches in the walls nearest them. Besides these, there were two wooden machines overlooking the top of the tower and the castle for crossbowmen and look-outs.

The most effective means of attack was under the wall by means of a mine. A tunnel would be dug until the foundations of a tower were reached. The stones were chipped away or burrowed under. The masonry would be held up by wooden props.

The space was then filled with anything which would burn such as straw, pitch and bacon fat. When everything was ready the attackers set light to the material. As the flames burnt through the wooden props the masonry above collapsed. The tower then came crashing down.

Usually mining was a last resort because it took a long time to carry out. This happened at the siege of Rochester Castle in 1215.

E Roger of Wendover, a monk of St Albans who died in 1236 wrote an account of the siege:
> King John did not allow the besieged any rest day or night. As well as the stones hurled from the catapults and slings and the missiles of the crossbowmen and archers, frequent attacks were made by the knights and their followers.
> At last the king used miners. Many of the royal troops had been killed and he saw his siege engines were useless. Soon the miners threw down a great part of the walls. The success of the miners in breaching the walls forced the defenders to retreat to the mighty square keep of the castle.

There are lots of different sources that historians can use. A historian needs to know what value to put on a source. He or she does this by asking questions about the sources.

C A modern artist's impression of a siege tower in use.

To go through the wall attackers had to use large catapults of various kinds. Two of them were the trebuchet and the mangonel. They were used to hurl heavy stones against points of weakness. A corner of a tower or a join in the wall were favourite targets. A battering ram might be used against the entrance gates.

D The Chronicle *Annals of Dunstable* gives a description of the capture of Bedford Castle in 1224 after a long eight-week siege:
> On the eastern side was a stone-throwing machine and two mangonels which attacked the new tower every day. On the western side were two mangonels which reduced

1. Look at sources A, B and C. In each case give the reasons for your answers.
   a) Which of the three sources is not as old as the scene it depicts?
   b) Does this mean that it is of little use as a source?
2. Which of the three sources gives us the most information
   (a) about weapons, (b) about armour and (c) about tactics?
3. Read sources D and E. Why did King John decide to use miners for the siege of Rochester Castle?
4. What difference is there between sources D and E?
5. How useful are sources D and E for finding out the ways in which castles were attacked?
6. How well do sources A, B and C support the information in D and E?

21

DEFENCE

The design of castles kept changing. Barons wanted to make their castles more and more difficult to attack. The first big improvement was when wooden defences were replaced with stone. At about the same time new towers called keeps were built. They were generally tall square blocks, with small towers in each corner.

A Rochester castle keep.

The base of most keeps was wider and sloped outwards so that large boulders would bounce away from the walls. The main entrance to the keep was normally on the first floor. It was approached by a flight of steps set at right angles to the door, running up the side of the wall.

The doorway was usually very narrow. This limited the number of attackers able to assault the door at any one time. Access to the other floors was by spiral staircases running up to the corner turrets.

The baileys were surrounded by stone walls. Small projecting towers were spaced along the wall. This meant that archers could fire arrows at any attackers who had managed to reach the foot of the wall.

Entrances to the bailey were likely to come under attack more than any other part of the castle. They had to be given extra protection. A strong gatehouse was built to protect the entrance. These usually had at least one portcullis. They could be lowered into position during an attack.

B These portcullises are at Hever Castle in Kent.

The entrance itself was like a tunnel through which any attacker had to pass. There were openings in the roof called 'murder holes'. Stones and other nasty things could be dropped onto the enemy's heads.

A square tower was particularly easy to bring down by mining. Later castles were built with round towers. They had several advantages. It reduced the number of blind points behind which attackers could hide. It removed the dangerous corners which were always points of weakness. A round tower was also better able to deflect boulders and other objects.

C The machicolations on the gatehouse of Carisbrooke Castle.

An additional defence was the machicolation. This stuck out from the top of the wall and had openings in the floor. These looked down directly on the wall beneath. The defenders could pour boiling oil straight down on the heads of the attackers. Sometimes a wooden platform with a roof, called a brattice, would be added.

The best designed castles were built in Wales by King Edward I. They included an outer line of massive walls with strong towers. This went round an inner ring of defences as strong as the first. The two rings of walls were often quite close. Attackers were faced by two sets of defenders. Even if attackers got through the outer wall and captured all its towers, the space between the walls became little more than a killing ground.

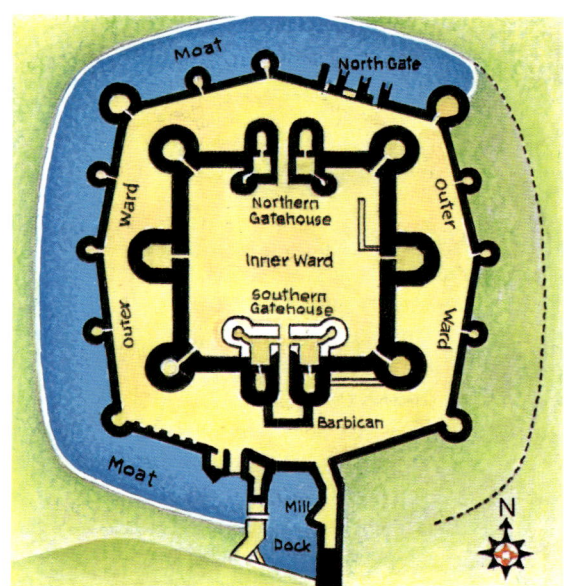

D Plan of Beaumaris Castle on Anglesey, built in the 1290s.

The layout of the defences made mining of the inner ring or the keep very difficult. Most of the castles built by Edward I were never taken by force. However, historians disagree on just how difficult it was to capture castles.

E Alan Reid writing in *Castles of Wales* (1973) says this:
> The vast majority of castles were very well equipped to resist attack and very few of them were carried by storm; [most] victories came as a result of starvation or treachery.

F On the other hand, J. and F. Gies, in their book *Life in a Medieval Castle* (1974), write:
> Hunger and thirst aside, no defensive fortification was proof against all attack, and even the strongest castles of the twelfth and thirteenth centuries could be, and were, captured.

It is important to realise that accounts of the past often disagree. This is sometimes because historians are only giving us their opinions of what happened. We can only decide whether we agree with either of the opinions by looking at the facts.

1. What does 'carried by storm' mean in source E?
2. What defensive fortifications does source F refer to?
3. Using the information in this chapter, what facts could you use to support source E?
4. In the same way, what facts could you use to support source F?

6 CATHEDRALS AS PLACES TO IMPRESS

BUILDING THE CATHEDRALS

Cathedrals were the biggest buildings in medieval England. They were also the most impressive buildings. They were designed to stand out. No expense was spared in using the best materials that money could buy. Every new cathedral had to be bigger and better than all the others. It also had to have the latest style of architecture.

Architects are people who design buildings. In the middle ages they were called master masons. They were different from architects because they were skilled craftsmen. They were also responsible for organising the workers.

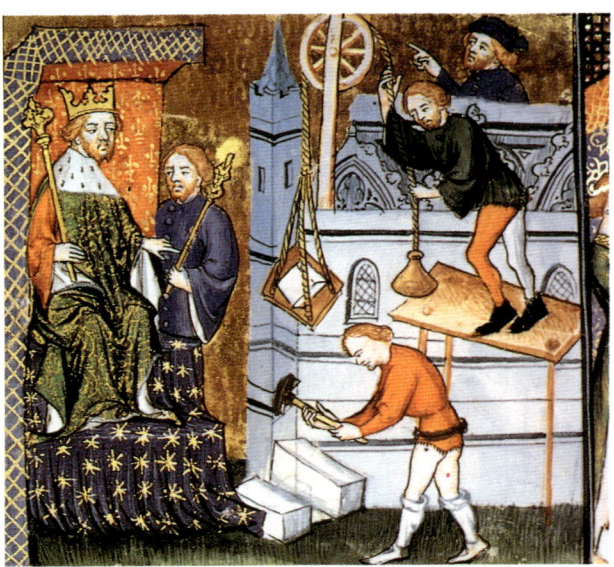

A Illustration from a 15th-century manuscript showing masons at work. The heavy stone blocks were lifted into place by wooden cranes.

The masons were the most important group of builders. They made the squared blocks of stone that the walls were built with. This was usually either limestone or sandstone. Sometimes it would be available from a nearby quarry. Otherwise the stone would have to be brought from another part of the country.

The mortar for binding the masonry together was made from a mixture of sand, lime and water. As the walls rose scaffolding was erected and special frames made to support the arches while the mortar set. The heavy stone blocks were lifted into place by cranes powered by people.

B An unusual view of the spire of Salisbury Cathedral seen from the inside, looking upwards through the framework of wooden scaffolding which was erected for the masons to work on in the 14th century.

Masons had to work a set number of hours each day. They also had to prove the quality of their work before they were taken on by the master mason.

C This is made clear by the Ordinances of the masons of York Minster in 1370:

> All their times and hours shall be ruled by a bell. No mason shall be accepted for work until he be first proved a week or more that he can work well. After he is found satisfactory in his work, he is to be accepted by the agreement of the master mason and the keepers of the work.

A large number of carpenters were needed. They put up the wooden scaffolding. But their main job was to put together the timber for the roof. The beams and rafters would be cut to size on the ground. When they were lifted to the roof they could be easily fitted together. The joints were held together with wedges and stout wooden pegs.

The beams holding up the roof had to be strong. This was because the roof was usually covered with lead, a very heavy metal. Plumbers were responsible for laying the sheets of lead. Glaziers also used lead. They were the craftsmen who made the windows. They used strips of lead to join together pieces of coloured glass to make up patterns.

The inside walls were covered in plaster. Once the plaster had dried, painters would cover the walls with pictures and decorations called murals. The painters would make their own paint. They also used paper-thin layers of real gold for parts of their murals.

Many other craftsmen were needed to work on various parts of the cathedral. These included brass founders, jewellers, silversmiths, goldsmiths and enamellers. These people would produce expensive furnishings for the altar. They would also decorate the shrine. Bell founders would cast the huge bells. Locksmiths made locks to keep the cathedral treasure safe.

Cathedrals took a long time to build, especially if progress was interrupted by war, plagues or accidents such as fires. The church at Durham was begun in 1093 and took about 40 years to complete. Peterborough, begun in 1117, took 70 years. Some cathedrals were never finished. This was usually because the money had run out.

Because the cathedrals were so big and took so long to complete, no one man could mastermind the whole work from beginning to end. A change of architect almost always meant a change of design. This is how the different styles of architecture came about.

D Masons still use the old tools.

1. How does the crane in source A work?
2. a) What would the carpenter have made in source A?
   b) What other things would the carpenter have made?
3. Why do you think masons still use the same tools today that medieval masons used?
4. Why would working on a medieval building site be fairly dangerous compared with today?

A Plan of Lincoln Cathedral, built between 1071 and 1546.

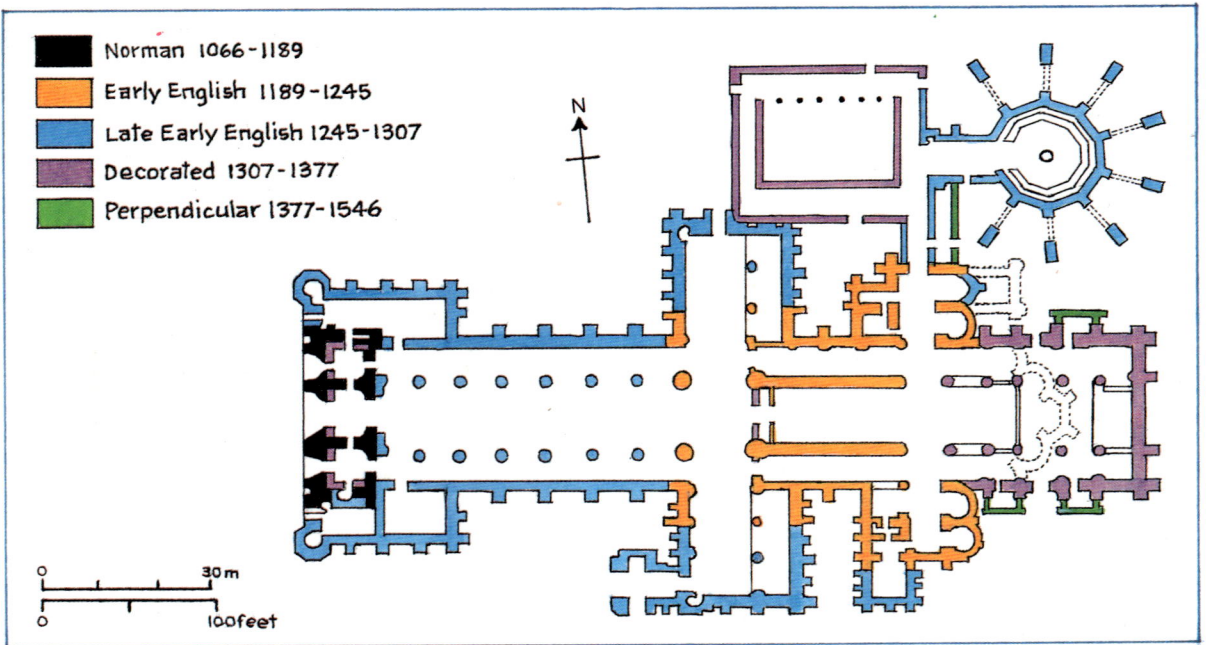

LINCOLN CATHEDRAL

When we want to find out about buildings the best way is to go and look at them. However, this is no good unless we know what to look for. If you know what to look for in a cathedral you can tell a lot about the history of it.

The first thing to realise is that most cathedrals were not all built at the same time. However, you can work out the age of a cathedral. The older ones were made in a different style of architecture to the later ones.

This sounds quite easy until you find out that you will usually see different styles of architecture in the same cathedral. This is because parts of the cathedral may have been rebuilt or extended. By knowing what to look for you can tell how the cathedral has changed throughout its history.

Lincoln Cathedral is an example of this. In 1071 William the Conqueror ordered a new cathedral to be built in Lincoln. At the same time he ordered the bishop to move from the little town of Dorchester to the larger town of Lincoln.

B The words on the charter of 1071 contain this order:
> William, king of the English, to Thorold the sheriff and to all the sheriffs of the diocese of Bishop Remigius, greeting. Know that I have transferred the seat of the bishop of Dorchester to the city of Lincoln by the authority and advice of Pope Alexander and also of Archbishop Lanfranc. I have given enough land there, free of all taxes, for the building of a mother church of the whole diocese and its other buildings.

Remigius, the new bishop, had helped William. He had persuaded his fellow monks in Normandy to give William a ship for his invasion of England and to hire knights to fight for him. Becoming a bishop was his reward.

The new cathedral was finished in 1092. It was 99 metres long with two square towers. The design was copied from cathedrals in Normandy. The only remains today are the lower part of the towers and the wall below them. The reason for this is that the roof was made of wood.

In 1141 there was a great fire which destroyed it. In order to keep up with the latest fashion the bishop rebuilt the roof in stone. Unfortunately this put too great a strain on the walls. They had been made to hold up only a timber roof.

In 1185 an earthquake gently shook the hill on which the cathedral stood. It was enough to bring down the greater part of Remigius' cathedral in ruins. After barely 100 years of life only the west front and towers were left standing.

A new bishop called Hugh arrived in 1186. He was determined to rebuild the cathedral. The first part to be built was for the choir and the altar. This is the most important part of the cathedral. The monks could not carry out their main job until this was done.

Gradually the work of rebuilding the cathedral continued. Eventually the nave joined the choir to the old west wall and towers. Cathedrals took a long time to build. Bishop Hugh died in 1200; he never saw the cathedral completed.

Over the next 300 years parts were added to the cathedral. During such a long time different styles of architecture came and went. It is these styles of architecture that tell us when parts of the cathedral were built. The plan of the cathedral (source A) shows when the separate parts were made. Each style had a different name.

D The Judgement Porch at Lincoln.

C The main door of Lincoln Cathedral.

The oldest part of the cathedral is, of course, Norman. The Norman style of architecture can be recognised by its round arches. Other features are thick columns holding up the roof with only small windows in the walls.

The later styles of architecture are called Gothic. Gothic arches are pointed. They are stronger than the Norman round arches. They made it possible to do without the solid walls of Norman cathedrals. The pillars are more slender. Also the windows are much larger. Compare sources C and D, both of which show doorways in Lincoln Cathedral built at different times.

History is about change. Change can be seen in different ways. The different styles of architecture are one way in which we can see change in the history of a cathedral.

1. Which source, C or D, is a Norman arch? Explain how you decided.
2. Look at source C. How can you tell that the row of kings was added after the archway was built?
3. Why were pointed arches stronger than round ones? Compare them using thin strips of card or paper.
4. List as many reasons as you can why Lincoln Cathedral has several different styles of architecture.

7 LIFE IN THE CASTLE

THE BUILDINGS

It is very difficult for us to imagine what it was like to live in a castle in medieval times. It must have been very different to the way we live now. We can imagine how cold and uncomfortable it was. But we need more than our imagination to get a real idea of what it was like.

We can look at the remains of castles that still exist but we still need a lot of imagination. However, there are plenty of clues to help us. One of the most impressive castles to survive is Rochester Castle. The keep at Rochester (source B) can tell us a lot about what it was like to live there.

You entered the keep through a guardroom (1) at the top of a steep flight of steps. You reached the different floors of the keep by a spiral staircase (2). There were two of these at opposite corners of the keep. The good thing about these was that they took up little space and they were easy to defend.

From the guardroom you entered the main part of the keep at the level of the first floor. Below this there was a storeroom for food and materials in case of a siege.

The main living quarters began on the first floor where the constable had his rooms. He was the person in charge of the castle. He had to look after it when the baron was away. The constable's hall was near the main door. This was where meals were served and where the constable gave out orders to the soldiers on duty in the castle. Some of the soldiers also slept in the constable's hall. The constable himself had his own bedroom beyond the hall.

The main floor of the castle was above the constable's room. Here there was the great hall (3) used by the Archbishop of Canterbury or the king when he came. The archbishop was also the baron who held Rochester Castle.

There was a gallery (4) around the top of the great hall. This was used by minstrels when they played on special occasions. It could also be used for extra sleeping space or for exercise during bad weather. The top floor contained the rooms reserved for the archbishop.

In all the main living rooms there were large fireplaces (5). These were set into the walls with chimneys going up through the outside walls of the keep. The windows of the main living rooms were larger than some of the others. They did not contain glass. Instead they were fitted with

A Inside the great hall at Rochester Castle. Notice the way arches have been decorated. Try to spot the well in the middle, the holes for the floor and the gallery at the top.

wooden shutters. They could be locked in place at night or when the castle was being attacked.

There was a well (6) going right through the middle of the castle. This was essential if the castle was going to survive a long siege. It could be used on all the floors of the keep. Toilets called garderobes were situated on each floor. They emptied into chutes which went through the outside wall of the keep.

There was a wallwalk (7) around the roof of the keep. This was patrolled to keep an eye on the surrounding countryside. The height of the keep, 34.5m, made it an excellent viewing place. There were holes for pigeons in the towers at the corners of the keep. They were part of the food supplies for the castle.

There was a chapel (8) above the guardroom. Below the guardroom was a prison. It so happens that underneath the floor of the prison there was a cesspit. Whether this was a way of torturing the prisoners is not clear!

Castles were uncomfortable by modern standards. One problem was that they had to be well fortified to resist attack. But they also had to provide a place for the baron and his household to live in some comfort.

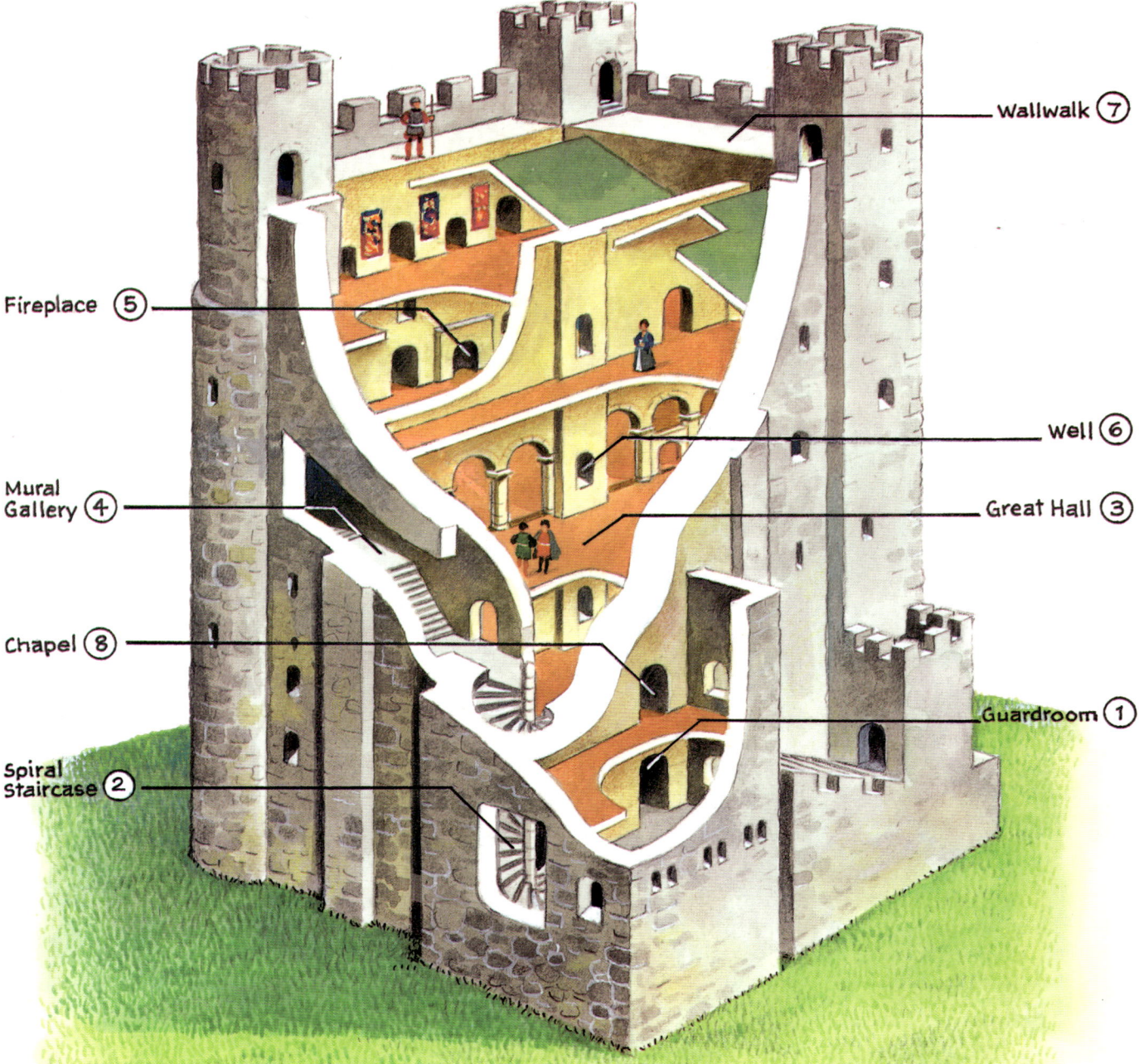

B Inside the keep at Rochester Castle.

C Gerald of Wales wrote about his family's castle of Manorbier in Pembrokeshire. Its attractive situation seemed as important as its military strength.

The castle is about three miles distant from Pembroke. It is excellently well defended by turrets and walls, and is situated on the summit of a hill extending on the western side towards the seaport. On the northern and southern sides it has a fine fish-pond under its walls, and a beautiful orchard on the same side, enclosed on one part by a vineyard, and on the other by trees. Between the castle and the church, near the site of a very large lake and mill, a stream of water flows through a valley.

This description sounds like an advertisement from an estate agent. No doubt Gerald could have given a glowing description of the inside of the castle. He would have mentioned the number of rooms, the heating arrangements, the decoration, water supply and toilet facilities.

1. a) List the things mentioned in the chapter and in source C which were provided to help the castle resist attack.
   b) List the things which helped to make the castle a home.

2. Write a description of a castle as if you were an estate agent trying to sell it to a wealthy baron.

A Preparing food is shown in this scene from the Luttrell Psalter. This was a religious book made for a 14th-century knight, Sir Geoffrey Luttrell. Although the writing is taken from the Bible, the pictures are scenes from the time when the book was made. Sources B, C and D are from the same book.

THE HOUSEHOLD

Besides the baron, his lady and their children, the household of a castle consisted of a number of staff. How many depended on how rich the lord was. Staff fell into two groups: the military and the domestic.

The military staff included household knights and knights from outside who were doing castle-guard duty. There were also squires, men-at-arms, a porter who guarded the outer door of the castle and watchmen.

The steward was in charge of the domestic staff. He looked after the day-to-day running of the castle. This included not only organising the servants, but also running the estate. The chamberlain looked after the great hall.

Several different servants had the job of preparing and serving the food eaten in the great hall. Apart from the cook, there was a pantler. He was in charge of the pantry. His name came from the French word *pain*, meaning *bread*. The butler (bottler) looked after the buttery where drink was kept in butts or bottles.

Feeding everybody in the castle was a big job. It was even more difficult if another baron was visiting. He would bring his own soldiers and servants with him. Extra supplies had to be brought in when this happened. It was worse if the king came to stay. No expense was spared to make sure the king was comfortable and well looked after.

C

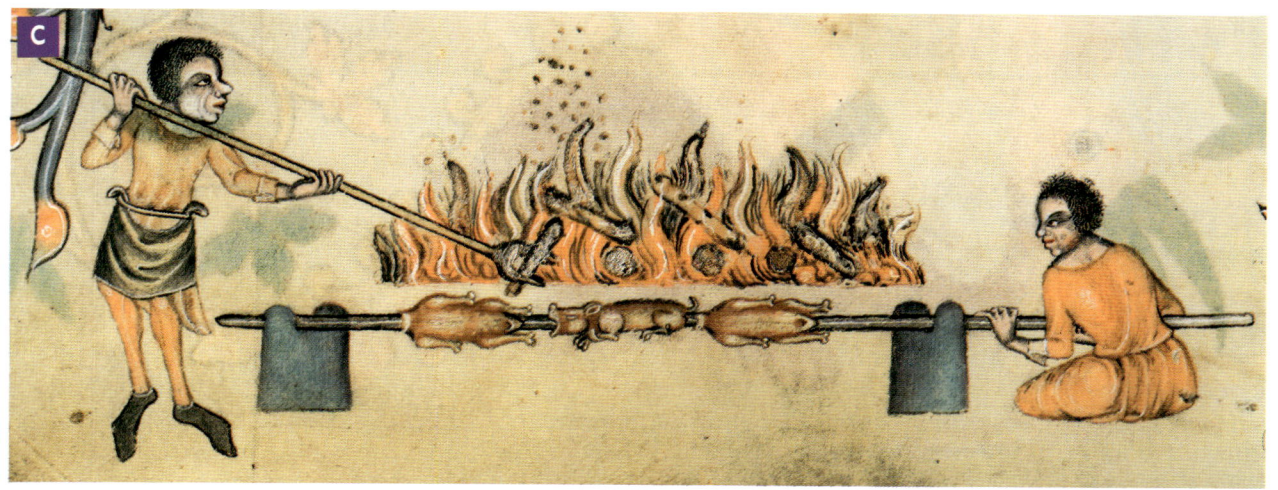

D

When trying to find out about life in the past, historians have to use whatever sources are available.

We are fortunate in having some household accounts showing what was bought. The earliest surviving accounts are those kept by Eleanor de Montfort. She was the wife of Simon de Montfort.

E Here is an entry for a Thursday in May 1265. (The usual daily wage of a skilled craftsman in the 13th century was about 4d (2p).)
On the Thursday following, for the Countess, at Portchester, R. de Bruce and A. de Montfort being present, with their household, and lord Simon's servants, and the garrison of the castle; bread bought, 8s (40p); wine, from stock. Kitchen. Meat bought, 2s 5d (12p), 6 sheep, and one cured hog from the stock of the castle. Eggs, 400, 18d (7p). Salt, 3d (1p).

1 a) Describe how the food is being cooked in sources A to C.
b) What types of meat are being served?
c) Which of the servants is likely to be the butcher?
d) Which servant is the man kneeling in front of the table? (Clue – he is watching the lord drink something.)
e) What is missing on the table which you would expect to see nowadays?

2 a) Which people mentioned in source E lived at Portchester Castle?
b) Which people mentioned in source E were visitors to Portchester Castle?

3 a) What kinds of information can we get from picture sources like A, B, C and D?
b) What can we learn from household accounts like source E?

31

8 LIFE IN THE ABBEY

THE BUILDINGS

There were over 1,000 monasteries in England. They varied a lot in size. But they all had one thing in common. Each one tried to supply the monks with all the needs of life within the walls of the monastery. The monks promised to devote their lives to God. They believed they could only do this by living in their own separate communities apart from the world.

Some of these monasteries were called abbeys. Others were called priories. Priories were generally smaller than abbeys and had a prior as head of the monastery. Castle Acre Priory was an example of this smaller type of monastery.

The church was the largest building in the priory. It stood on the north side of the monastery site. This was to provide a shelter against the colder winds. It was shaped like a cross. The chancel was at the east end of the church. Here it would catch the morning sunlight.

The monk's burial ground was on the north side of the church. On the south was the cloister. This was a covered passage-way each side of a square courtyard. The cloister had several uses. It was a passage linking important parts of the monastery. It was a place where the monks could get some exercise under cover.

It was also a place for the monks to study. In some monasteries, small carrels were put along the south side. Here each monk had a desk where he could read and write. Other parts of the cloister might have wooden cupboards built into the wall for storing books. There might be statues of saints to give the monks examples to follow.

The chapter house was on the eastern side of the cloister. The monks met here every morning. Inside the chapter house the prior sat on a special chair. The monks sat in benches around the walls.

The meeting was important because it kept everyone in touch with what was going on. The monks discussed the running of the monastery. Sometimes they would talk about business matters. If a monk was accused of breaking the Rule and found guilty, his punishment was decided by the prior. Punishments could include being put on a diet of bread and water. For serious offences a monk was put in the monastery prison.

A An old monk of Durham wrote about this in a book called the *Rites of Durham* in 1593:
> There was a strong prison which was made for all those who were great offenders. If any of the monks had been found guilty of any crime he had to stay in the prison for one whole year in chains.

B Aerial photograph of Castle Acre Priory.

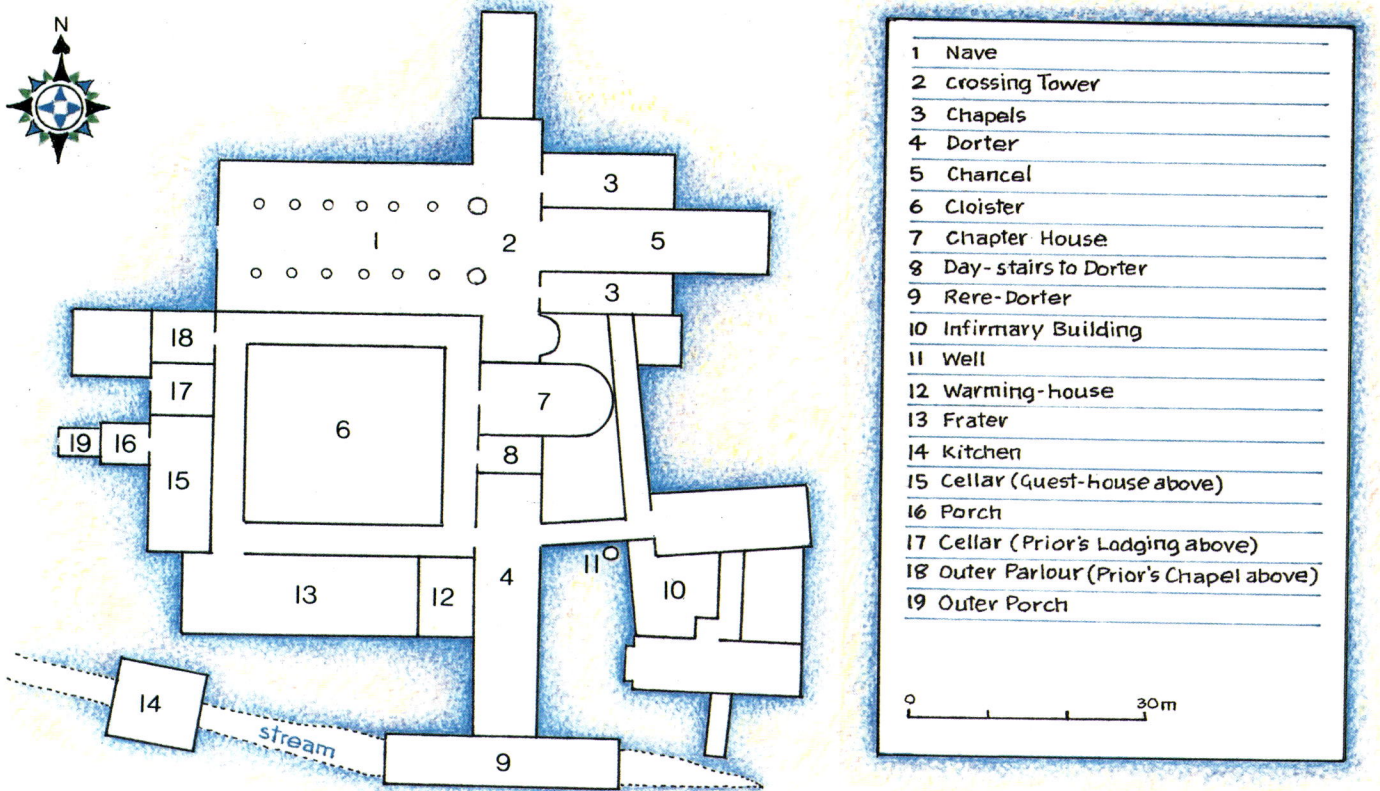

C Plan of Castle Acre Priory.

Near the chapter house was the monks' dormitory called the dorter. This was a large room with rows of beds. The rere-dorter was next to the dorter. This was the monks' lavatory; it had the luxury of a proper drain!

The refectory (or frater) was on the southern side of the cloister. Here the monks ate their meals. Built into the wall of the refectory there was a pulpit. This was a raised platform where a monk would read to the others while they were eating.

Next to the refectory was the warming-house. This was the only place where the monks were allowed to come and warm themselves in cold weather. The church and the other main parts of the priory were unheated.

The prior had his own rooms. At Castle Acre it was inside the monastery itself. Elsewhere, it might be a separate house outside the monastery. If the prior often entertained important guests, his house would have several rooms. Less important guests and travellers would stay in a separate guest house.

Other buildings included the infirmary for the sick and old monks. Most monks spent a few days every year in the infirmary. This was because of the practice of blood-letting. We would think it an unpleasant operation. It involved cutting the flesh and letting the blood collect in a bowl. Another method was to apply leeches to the skin and allow them to suck your blood.

Monks looked forward to this because they were allowed three days' rest in the infirmary afterwards. This meant getting up late, plenty of meat and rich food, and no work.

> Much information can be gained from looking at the remains of monasteries. Although they are mostly in ruins, it is possible to work out a lot from what is left.

1. Look carefully at sources B and C. Using the plan, work out what you can see on the photograph.
   a) Which two parts of Castle Acre Priory still have their roofs?
   b) Give a reason why the rere-dorter is built where it is.
   c) Which part of the priory would visitors first enter? Explain how you decided.
   d) How does the position of the cloister tell you that it was an important part of the monastery?
   e) Apart from in the warming-house, where else would there probably be a fire?
2. Stone is all that remains of the monastery. Does this mean that all the buildings were made of stone? Give reasons for your answer.
3. What does source A tell you that the remains of the buildings alone could not?

THE ABBOT AND HIS MONKS

Anybody wanting to become a monk or nun had to be over 17 years old. When you entered the monastery you did not become a monk straight away. You became a novice. You had to give up all your property to the monastery or to the poor.

Your own clothes would be kept. This was in case you changed your mind and decided to leave. After 12 months you made three solemn promises. You promised not to marry, not to own any possessions, and to do whatever the head of the monastery told you.

All the monks made the same promises. They all knew their main task was to worship God. However, there were several different jobs that a monk might do.

The abbot or abbess was head of the monastery. In the smaller monasteries he or she was called a prior or prioress. In some of the large cathedrals like Durham, the bishop was also the abbot. He was usually too busy to spend any time in the monastery of the cathedral. Here, too, the monastery was ruled by a prior.

A A 13th-century picture of a monk called Hugh of Saint-Victor.

The sacristan was in charge of the abbey church. He had to make sure the church was cleaned. He saw to the lighting of the church. This was necessary because a lot of the services were carried out by the monks while it was still dark. He also had to look after all the fixtures and decorations in the church. This included especially the altars and shrines.

B A manuscript illustration of a monk at work.

The precentor was in charge of all the books. This was an important job because books were very valuable. Each one was written out by hand. They were beautifully decorated, often with jewelled covers of leather. They were some of the monastery's most prized possessions. The precentor's job also included leading the singing at services.

The cellarer had a very big job. He was in charge of the property of the abbey. This included its lands and money. He also kept the kitchen, the bakery and the brewery supplies. He saw to any repairs to the buildings.

C This extract from the Accounts of the Cellarers of Battle Abbey for 1441 gives some idea of the things the cellarer had to do:

For various wooden hoops bought for mending containers and pipes within the monastery, 26s 10d (£1.34). For cutting 350 wagon loads of firewood, 45s 6d (£2.28). For carters hired for carting the firewood, 17s 9d (88p). For various men hired for mending the roads to Bodiam and Bathurst for the carting of hay and wood. For making two wheelbarrows, 6d (2p) and one wheel for the same, 9d (3p). For 1lb (0.45kg) of onions bought in London for sowing in the garden, 4d (2p). For the servants' presents at Christmas and Easter, 6s (30p).

The almoner gave money, food and clothing to the poor. Every day he met people from outside the monastery.

D Commissioners who reported on the monasteries in 1536 had this to say about the nunnery of St. Mary's, Winchester:

Great help is daily given to the inhabitants of the city.

E At Ulverscroft they reported that:

The monastery stands in a wilderness in Charnwood Forest. It gives refreshments to many poor people and gypsies.

The novice-master trained the novices. They had to learn about the duties of a monk.

F The monk who wrote the *Rites of Durham* in 1593 remembered the part of the monastery where the novices were taught:

Near the treasure house door, there was a big wooden stall where the novices sat and learnt. Also the master of the novices had a carved wooden seat next to the stall where the novices sat and looked at their books. There he sat and taught the novices both in the morning and afternoon.

G The same writer recalls that the novices were given some free time:

There was belonging to the common room a bowling alley at the back for the novices sometimes to play when they had permission from their master. He stood by to see they kept good order.

The hosteller looked after the guests of the monastery. Some large monasteries had plenty of space for guests.

H The monk who wrote the *Rites of Durham* was very proud of the welcome given to visitors:

There was a famous house of hospitality called the guest hall in the abbey yard of Durham. The entertainment was as good as any in England, both for the quality of the food and the fine furniture in the bedrooms.

I Manuscript illustration showing a monk from Canterbury at work.

J The amount of time monks spent in the different parts of the monastery would vary. A typical day was as follows. (Services are named in red.)

Midnight	Matins in the church (about one hour)
	Then back to bed
6 a.m.	Prime in the church (about ½ hour)
	Breakfast
	Work or reading
9 a.m.	Chapter Mass in the church
10 a.m.	Chapter meeting in the Chapter house
11 a.m.	High Mass in the church
12 noon	Dinner
	Then siesta
2 p.m.	Nones in the church (about ½ hour)
	Work
4 p.m.	Vespers in the church (about ½ hour)
	Work
6 p.m.	Supper
7 p.m.	Compline in the church (about ½ hour)
	Then to bed (later in summer)

1 a) Make a list of the different parts of the monastery mentioned in the chapter.
b) On a scale of 1 to 10, write down next to each part in your list how much time an ordinary monk might spend there. For instance, the monks would spend a lot of time in the church so you would give it 9 or 10. You will need to look at source J.

2 a) For sources A, B and I, describe what the monks are doing.
b) What job do you think the monk in source A had?
c) Why did the monk in source I need a knife as well as a pen?

3 Do the pictures tell us more about life in the monastery than the actual remains of the monasteries? Explain your answer.

9 THE CASTLES OF EDWARD I

1000　　　1100　　　1200　　　1300　　　1400　　　1500

THE CONQUEST OF WALES

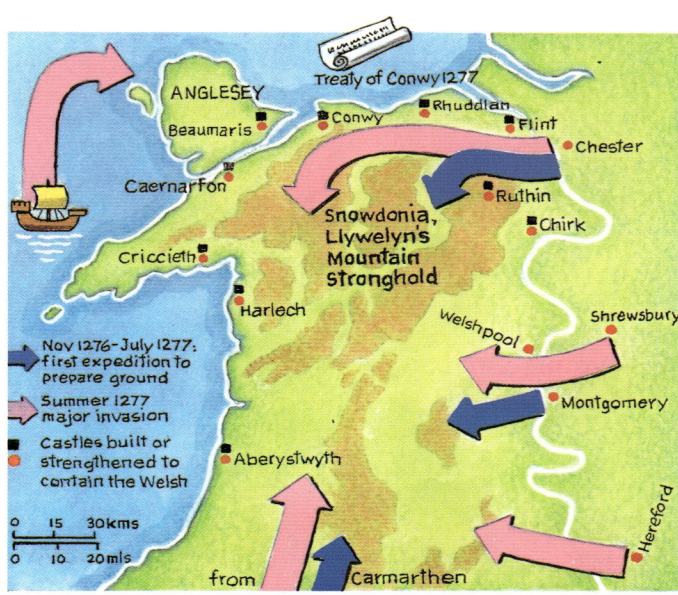

A Map of Edward I's invasion of Wales.

At Cilmeri, a mile-and-a-half west of the country town of Builth Wells in Powys, stands a roadside monument. It commemorates Llywelyn ap Gruffyd, the last of the native Welsh princes.

Llywelyn had tried to gain independence from the English. At first he was fairly successful. King Henry III recognised Llywelyn as Prince of Wales. When Henry died Edward I became king.

First, Llywelyn annoyed Edward by marrying the daughter of Simon de Montfort. Simon was the rebel baron who had troubled Henry III. Secondly, Llywelyn refused to attend Edward's coronation or his parliament at Westminster.

In 1277 Llywelyn was declared a rebel. The English army marched into Wales. Edward attacked from Chester, Montgomery and Carmarthen (see source A). Edward himself went with the army advancing along the coast of north Wales from Chester. At Flint, Edward built a castle which served as a base camp.

B This was recorded by a monk called Thomas Wykes in his chronicle for 1277:
> Edward immediately began the building of two castles. They were heavily fortified to suit the flat terrain on the banks of the River Clwyd. They provided safe quarters for himself and his men. One of the castles was called Flint, the other Rhuddlan.

By the end of July 1277 there was an army of builders at Flint. There were one master engineer, 970 diggers under three masters, 330 carpenters, 320 woodmen, 200 masons under a master, 12 smiths and ten charcoal-burners.

Each group was commanded by a knight, who kept discipline. He was helped by a royal clerk, who dealt with finding workers and paying them.

The numbers increased with the arrival of 300 diggers from Lincolnshire. They came under the escort of three mounted sergeants, who stopped them deserting on the way. By the end of August there were 2,300 diggers alone. The cost of all this was enormous. At Flint the bill was around £7,000.

Steadily advancing along the coast, Edward cut off Llywelyn from his supply base on Anglesey. The key to Edward's success was his use of the navy which supplied his army as it moved forward.

C Thomas Wykes wrote about Llywelyn's surrender in his chronicle:
> Sturdy sailors from the Cinque Ports with a large fleet of ships, landed on the island near to Snowdonia called Anglesey and seized it. Prince Llywelyn, by now bewildered and defeated, surrendered himself and his land to [the king].

D Rhuddlan Castle as it is today.

E Ships loading stores from a 14th-century manuscript.

At the Treaty of Conwy, Llywelyn was allowed to keep Snowdonia. However, this marked only a pause in the fighting. In 1282 Llywelyn attacked again.

F A monk from Worcester wrote this in his chronicle for the year 1282:
> In this tenth year of King Edward's reign, at dead of night on Palm Sunday [21 March], Llywelyn, Prince of Wales, and Daffyd, his brother, lay siege to Rhuddlan and Flint castles with a large army.

Edward was quick to put down this uprising. Llywelyn was killed in combat on 11 December 1282. Daffyd was captured not long after.

G The monk from Worcester recorded his fate:
> The death of a traitor is indeed shameful! Daffyd was dragged at a horse's tail through the streets of Shrewsbury, then hanged and finally decapitated. Afterwards, his body was hacked into four portions, his heart and intestines were burned and his head taken to London, to be displayed on the stake at the Tower, next to his brother's head. The four quarters of his headless corpse were sent to Bristol, Northampton, York and Winchester.

Edward was determined that no other rebel would unite the Welsh. So he carried out the greatest programme of castle building ever undertaken. He spent £100,000 on ten new royal castles – Builth, Aberystwyth, Flint, Rhuddlan, Ruthin, Hope, Conwy, Harlech, Caernarfon and Beaumaris.

Edward was an expert in castle building. He surveyed every site personally and was usually present when the work began. Of course Edward did not design and build the castles himself. He employed one of the greatest architects of the middle ages – James of St George.

The ten royal castles built by James vary a lot in design and appearance. But they have certain features in common. All were near to the sea or tidal rivers. This was to take advantage of Edward's complete naval supremacy. Wherever possible, they had docks, as at Beaumaris.

Another common feature was the use of the latest ideas for defence. They were so well designed that even the larger castles could be defended by just a few men. For instance, Conwy is a very large and powerful castle. But it needed only 30 people to defend it. There were 15 crossbowmen, a chaplain, a smith, a craftsman, a carpenter, a mason and ten others, mostly watchmen.

---

1. a) Why do you think Flint and Rhuddlan were built on the banks of the River Clwyd?
   b) Why were diggers needed at Flint?
   c) Why did Flint and Rhuddlan have to be heavily fortified?
2. Is there any evidence that some of the diggers were forced to work? Explain your answer.
3. Why did Edward have to advance along the coast?
4. Why do you think parts of Daffyd's body were sent to different parts of the kingdom?
5. a) How would you explain Edward's success in conquering Wales? Make a list of your reasons.
   b) Which reason would you say was the most important? Explain how you decided.

CAERPHILLY CASTLE

A The west gateway of Caerphilly Castle.

The largest castle in Wales is not a royal castle. Caerphilly Castle was built in 1268 for Gilbert de Clare. It covers 30 acres and stands on an island, surrounded by a lake.

It was the first concentric castle in Britain. This means that it had a double set of defences. The concentric plan was designed as protection against better siege weapons. Even if an enemy got through the first line of walls, he would not be able to get any further. He would be trapped in the space between the two walls. He could be killed by the soldiers on the second line. This was taller and overlooked the first line.

At Caerphilly it was even difficult to get anywhere near the walls. Not only had you to cross a lake, but the main gate was defended by a long wall with several towers. All the gateways have portcullises, 30 in total.

Inside the inner wall there is a passage going all round the castle. Soldiers armed with crossbows used this passage to get quickly to the side of the castle being attacked.

Small entrances called sallyports were made on the northern and southern sides of the castle. This meant supplies could be brought into the castle by boat. They also provided openings through which counter-attacks could be launched.

B Aerial view of Caerphilly Castle.

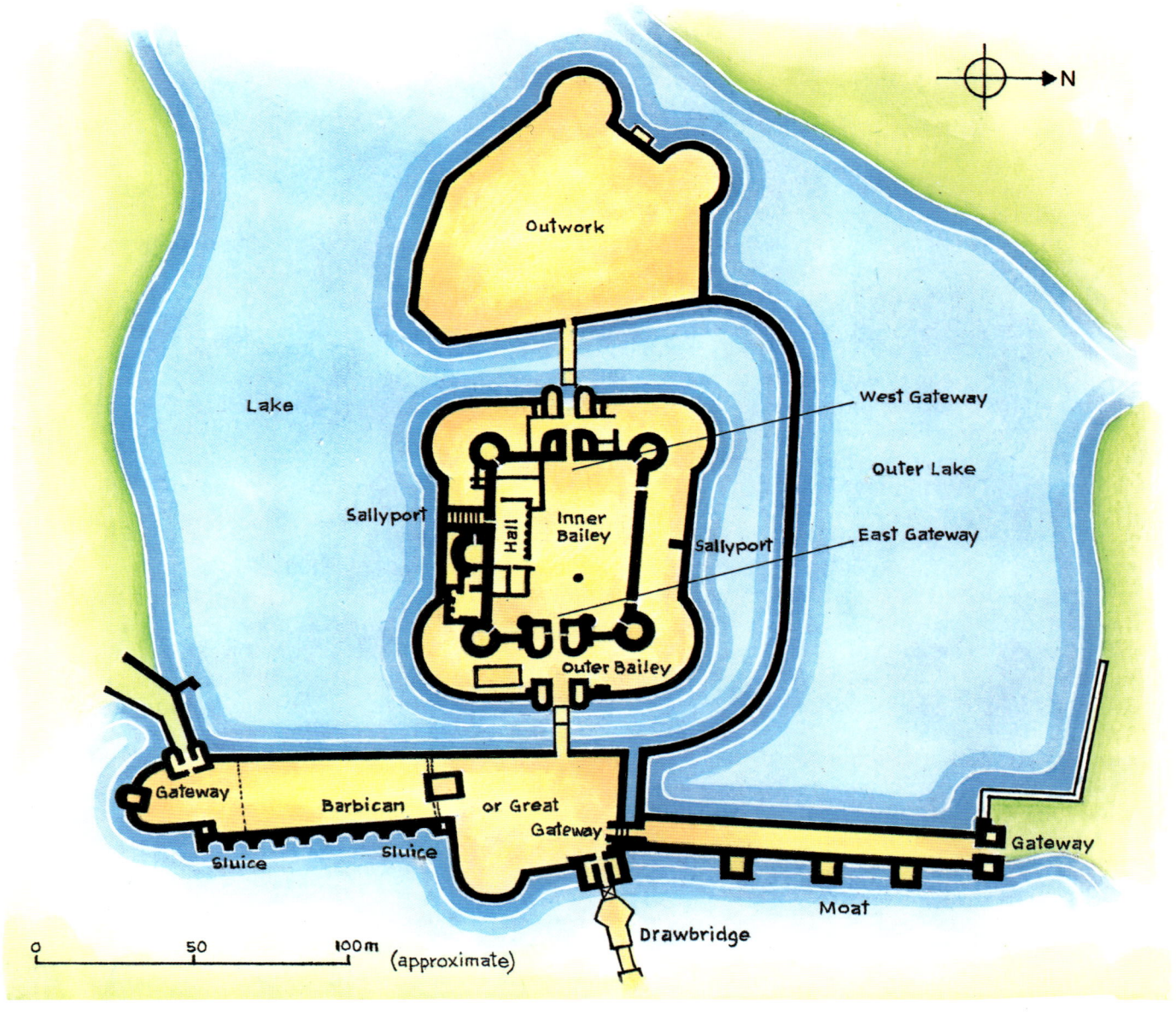

C Plan of Caerphilly Castle.

1. a) What was the first line of defence that had to be overcome by anyone attacking Caerphilly Castle?
   b) What was the second line of defence?
   c) What was the third line of defence?
2. a) How many drawbridges did you have to cross if you entered the castle from the east?
   b) What part of the castle would be the last to surrender?
3. Suppose attackers got through either of the gateways at the ends of the long wall. Why was it likely that many would be killed before they got to the drawbridge into the main part of the castle?
4. Here is a list of different ways of attacking the castle:
   (i) Go through the main gateways making your own bridges and burning down the portcullises.
   (ii) Cross the lake on rafts and scale the walls.
   (iii) Dig a tunnel under the lake and capture the outwork.
   (iv) Use catapults to hurl rotting animal bodies into the castle to spread disease.
   (v) Wait patiently until the castle ran out of food.
   (vi) Smuggle spies into the castle to open the drawbridges and gates from the inside.
   a) Write down the list with the method you think most likely to succeed at the top and the method you think the least likely to succeed at the bottom. You may add any other ideas of your own.
   b) Explain one advantage and one disadvantage of each method.

10 THE MONKS OF FOUNTAINS ABBEY

| 1000 | 1100 | 1200 | 1300 | 1400 | 1500 |

The first monks were followers of St Benedict who in 529 founded the great abbey of Monte Cassino in Italy. He wrote a set of rules for monks called the Benedictine Rule. The Rule meant that the monks were expected to devote their lives to the service of God.

The abbey of St Mary at York was one of the most successful Benedictine monasteries in England. By 1132 it had become wealthy and powerful. The monks had settled down to an easy way of life. However, some of the monks said that this was wrong. They thought that the monks should keep to their vow of poverty.

Six of the monks started to discuss what they could do about it. They asked their prior for advice. He said that he shared their views. He was even prepared to put their case to the abbot.

Abbot Geoffrey was then an old man, well-meaning but set in his ways. He could not accept that a small group of his monks had any right to put forward their own ideas. Discussions dragged on into the autumn with nothing settled. Meanwhile the original six had grown to 13. They included the prior, sub-prior, sacristan, precentor and almoner.

Finally, Prior Richard took their case to the Archbishop of York. When the archbishop arrived at the abbey to discuss the problem, he was prevented from entering the chapter house by monks who still supported the abbot. A fight broke out and the 13 rebel monks took shelter in the church.

The archbishop wanted to help them so he allowed them to stay at his palace until something was decided. Eventually, two days after Christmas 1132, the archbishop led the monks to some waste land in the deserted valley of the River Skell in a remote part of Yorkshire. There were springs of good water in the rocky sides of the valley, and so the monks chose to call their new abbey *Fountains*.

They elected Prior Richard as their first abbot. They were now on their own. The monks, in the depths of winter, had only the clothes on their backs and a store of bread left by the archbishop. The bitter winter was spent sheltering first under the rocks and then under a great elm tree. Gradually they cleared land for a garden and built a hut and a chapel.

When the winter was over the monks decided to join the Cistercian order of monks. The Cistercians believed it was important to give up all wealth and luxury. They refused all personal comforts. They would not wear cloaks, shirts or warm bedclothes. They did not even allow combs for their hair. The abbot was expected to share the hardships of the ordinary monks.

A The monks at Fountains Abbey had to clear large areas of woodland for their sheep pastures. This is a capital letter I from a 12th-century manuscript.

B The Cistercians employed large numbers of lay brothers. This is a capital letter Q from a 12th-century manuscript.

C Fountains Abbey still looks impressive today.

Despite the help they had received from the archbishop, the monks had no other support. During the first years the monks nearly starved several times. On one occasion they were forced to live on soup made from elm leaves.

By 1135 their position was so desperate that Abbot Richard decided to move the monastery to France. However, at the last moment they were saved. Hugh, Dean of York, had retired to end his days at the abbey. He brought with him his library and plenty of money. His example was followed by others.

The monks of Fountains became famous for the strict way they kept to their religious vows. Their number grew rapidly and some of the monks set out to start new abbeys elsewhere. They began to make permanent buildings. As more and more people gave land to the abbey, it became the richest Cistercian monastery in England.

The main source of its great wealth was wool. By 1300, Fountains had become the largest producer of wool in the north with more than 15,000 sheep. Each year the flocks were brought down from the high ground to be sheared. The wool was carried by packhorse and by boat to York for sale.

> History is made by people and the things they have done. Their actions are often caused by their ideas and attitudes.

1. a) What caused the 13 monks to break away in 1132?
   b) Did they believe that their actions were based on new ideas? Give the reasons for your answer.
   c) What vow were they breaking?
   d) What reasons would they have given for breaking this vow?
   e) Why did Abbot Geoffrey want things to stay as they were?
2. What would have happened if the monks had kept their ideas to themselves? Explain your answer.
3. a) How did things change for the monks who started Fountains Abbey?
   b) Do you think these changes made any differences to the monks' ideas? Explain your answer.

11 NUNS

Before you leave school or college you will take some time choosing a job. This can be difficult, but there is a wide choice available to both boys and girls. In the middle ages things were very different. There were very few choices and most boys and girls would do very much the same work as their parents.

For most girls, marriage and having children were the accepted aims in life. If you were a girl from a wealthy family there was an alternative – you could become a nun. Your parents had to be fairly well off. They had to pay the nunnery an amount of money called a dowry before their daughter was admitted as a novice.

There were many reasons why girls were willing to go into nunneries. Some women did wish to devote their lives to religion. Others saw it as a good career. Not all girls became nuns willingly. Some were sent to a convent by relatives who wanted to take over the wealth they had inherited.

A Robert de Playce in 1345 left money in his will for his niece to go into a convent. It is not clear whether she wanted to:

> I give to the daughter of John de Playce, my brother, 100s (£5) in silver, to help her become a nun in one of the houses of Wickham, Yedingham or Muncton.

B Nuns taking part in a church service, in about 1300. The fifth nun from the left is carrying a crozier.

C This nun is spinning wool.

The life of a nun was supposed to be as strict as that of monks. Nuns did all the same jobs as the monks. The only exception to this rule was that no women were allowed to become priests.

Some of the names for the different jobs were very similar as well. There was the abbess or prioress as head of the convent. They were responsible for discipline and order. The chantress trained the nuns to sing well. The sacrist was in charge of preparing everything in the church. These jobs were important because the nuns spent so much time singing in the church.

Other nuns looked after the housework. A nun called the fractress took care of all the eating arrangements. The cellaress actually ordered the food.

D At Syon Abbey in 1536 these were the orders for the cellaress:

> The cellaress shall buy meat and drink, ordering for the bakehouse, kitchen, buttery, pantry, cellar and such other.

All these different jobs meant that the nuns had plenty of work to keep them busy. The smooth running of the convent relied on the nuns doing their jobs properly.

However, just as with monks, girls did not always enter a convent for religious reasons. Some did not take the services seriously. This sometimes meant that the nuns went through the services as quickly as possible. Some nuns even took their pets into the church with them, even though this was strictly forbidden.

E When the Bishop of Winchester was inspecting a nunnery in 1387 he had this to say:
> We have convinced ourselves by clear proof that some of the nuns in your house bring with them to church, birds, rabbits, hounds, and such things. They pay more attention to them than to the service.

Other rules broken by nuns included the wearing of jewellery which was not allowed. No doubt women from rich families found it difficult to give up such things.

F According to a bishop visiting Ankerwyke priory in 1441 the Prioress wore:
> very expensive golden rings with precious stones. Also silver belts and silk veils. She wears furs and round her neck a long cord of silk with a gold diamond ring hanging on it.

Another reason why nuns might have been fashion conscious was that they came into contact with women from outside the nunnery. This was very likely to happen if the nuns had rich widows staying in the convent.

In several other ways the nuns had dealings with the outside world. Most larger convents employed servants to do the cooking and the housework. The nuns also had to manage their estates which meant they had to be good at business. Many of the local peasants worked on land owned by the convent.

The peasants also looked to the nuns in hard times. The giving of alms was an important part of the nuns' work.

H At Lacock Abbey the nuns recorded:
> We ought to feed on All Soul's day as many as there are nuns. To each poor person a dry loaf with two herrings or a slice of cheese.

By 1350 there were 256 convents, containing about 3,300 nuns. This compared with about 14,000 monks. Most nunneries were priories. There were 19 abbeys for nuns.

Some books give the impression that nuns were very serious people. We are led to believe that they spent all their time shut in from the outside world. It may be true that some nuns devoted their whole lives to the worship of god. Was this the case for most nuns?

---

1. a) Look at source B. What are the four nuns on the left holding?
   b) What are the other three nuns doing?
   c) What position in the convent did the nun holding a crozier have?
   d) What do you think is on the altar in the bottom right-hand corner of the picture?
2. Why did the nuns need to have monks in the church for their services?
3. What rule is the nun in source C breaking?
4. What differences are there between the impression of nuns you get from the sources compared with the normal view of nuns? Explain your answer fully.

G These nuns appear to be breaking several rules!

12 FRIARS

Friars were the followers of St Francis. He came from a rich family. One day, in 1207, he realised that he was wasting his life in idleness and pleasure. He decided to give up everything and live like a beggar. He did all this in the name of Jesus.

Some people were so impressed by his example that they decided to follow his example. They called themselves friars. They were known as Franciscans from the name of their founder.

A A picture of a friar from a 14th-century manuscript.

There were also friars called Dominicans from the name of *their* founder, St Dominic. Both Dominic and Francis gave importance to the help of women in their work. One of Francis' early followers was St Clare who ran away from home at the age of 18 in 1212. She started an order of nuns called the Poor Clares. She led her nuns for 40 years. For much of this time she suffered from serious ill-health caused by her harsh way of life.

The friars lived in extreme poverty, begging for food. They had no possessions apart from one habit, one belt of cord and one pair of breeches. They had no shoes and travelled barefoot even on the coldest winter days.

B An example of this is this story told by Brother Thomas Eccleston in his Chronicle (1258):
It chanced that Brother Walter of Madeley had found a pair of sandals. He had put them on when he went to Matins. But later when he had gone to bed, he dreamed that he had to go through a dangerous valley between Oxford and Gloucester. Robbers were known to operate there.

When he came down into the deep valley, robbers ran up to him from either side of the road. They were shouting, saying, "Kill, kill!" Greatly terrified, he said he was a friar. But they replied, "You lie, for you are wearing sandals."

Friars first came to England in 1224. They soon grew in numbers and became a common sight throughout the country. But they were slow to build their own churches. In fact, their rules forbade them to own buildings. When some friars were given a stone-built house in Shrewsbury to live in, they tore it down and put mud huts in its place.

The monks saw the friars as rivals. In some towns the monks attempted to turn them away. In Bury St Edmunds the friars tried to invade the town by night. They even brought a portable altar with them. The monks eventually managed to get them to leave.

C Some friars carried portable altars like this one.

D Matthew Paris, a monk of St Albans Abbey, wrote about the friars in his Chronicle for the year 1243:
Only 24 years after their beginning, they were building their first houses in England. Within the high walls of costly buildings, growing larger daily, they set out priceless treasures.

Matthew knew that the friars were supposed to believe in poverty. So he was able to criticise them for accepting gifts.

E Matthew accused the friars of more than just accepting gifts:

> When great and rich men lay dying, the friars would be in urgent attendance, greedy for money, to the loss and hurt of the clergy.

F Friars and devils. A late 14th-century manuscript criticising friars.

> Before we believe what people have written we need to know why they wrote what they did. Often they give us a one-sided view.

1. a) Why should we be careful about believing sources D and E?
   b) What are the friars being accused of in source E?
   c) What words in source E give us a clue to the real reason why Matthew criticised the friars?

Monks did not always complain about the friars. Matthew mentions how the prioress of the small Benedictine nunnery of Markyate near Luton helped the Dominicans of Dunstable on their arrival with a daily gift of loaves.

There are several sources that point to the real hardship suffered by some friars.

G This is an example from 1528:

> The city of Shrewsbury grants £5 to the friars because of the great poverty and ruin of their house. In return the friars promise their prayers.

H Other sources support the views of the monks. This is part of a poem written in the early 14th century:

> If a poor man come to a friar to ask for his blessing,
> And there come a richer man who brings a gift,
> He is shown into the refectory and looked after,
> And the poor man is kept standing outside,
> He is not seen to until the next day.

Yet some friars did take their religion very seriously. Some were even willing to die for it. This happened to one friar called John Stone. He disagreed with Henry VIII who wanted to get rid of the friars. He was executed in 1539.

I This is the expense account for his execution in Canterbury:

> Item paid for half a ton of timber to make a pair of gallows for to hang friar Stone 2s 6d (12p)
> Item paid to a carpenter for making the gallows 16d (7p)
> Item paid to a labourer that digged the holes 3d (1p)
> Item paid to four men to help set up the gallows 7d (4p)
> Item paid for drink for them 1d (less than 1p)
> Item paid for the carriage of the timber 4d (2p)
> Item paid for a hurdle 6d (3p)
> Item paid for a load of wood and a horse to pull him to the dungeon 2s 3d (11p)
> Item paid to two men that fetched the kettle and parboiled him 12d (5p)
> Item paid to three men that carried his quarters to the gates and set them up 13d (6p)
> Item paid for a noose to hang him 1d (less than 1p)
> Item paid to a woman that scoured the kettle 2d (1p)
> Item paid to him that did the execution 4s 8d (24p)
> He was cut down before he was dead. Then his intestines were pulled out.

> Our ideas about the past depend on what sources historians use. Sometimes they only choose sources which support their ideas. A balanced account usually has sources giving both sides of the argument.

2. a) Which sources would you use to give a bad opinion of the friars? Explain your choice.
   b) Which sources would you use to give a good opinion of the friars? Again, explain your choice.
3. Using information from the sources, write two descriptions of friars:
   a) giving a bad impression of them.
   b) giving a good impression of them.
4. Read source I. Using this information, write your own account of how John Stone was executed.

13 CHIVALRY

A Tilting at the quintain from a 14th-century manuscript.

HOW TO BECOME A KNIGHT

If you wanted to become a knight you had to be of noble birth – and a boy! At the age of seven you were sent away to live in the castle of a knight chosen by your parents. Here you worked as a page in the knight's household. Your main job was to run errands. At the same time you were given the chance to learn horsemanship and the use of weapons.

One way of learning how to fight on horseback was by constant practice in tilting at the quintain. This was a post with a rotating cross-bar. On one end of the bar there was a shield. On the other end there was a sandbag which would swing round and strike an unskilful rider. You were also expected to be good at running, boxing, wrestling and fencing.

As well as learning about fighting, you had to learn how to behave in polite company.

B An example of this is in *The Babees Book* written around 1475:
> Take no seat, but be ready to stand until you are asked to sit down. Keep your hands and feet at rest; do not claw your flesh or lean against a post, in the presence of your lord, or handle anything belonging to the house.
> Be respectful to your lord always when you answer; otherwise, stand as still as a stone, unless he speaks to you.

At about the age of 14, if you had made good progress, you would be promoted to the rank of squire. Your training would now become more demanding.

You also took on more duties. These included attending your master when he dressed and undressed, making his bed, and keeping your master's armour and weapons in perfect condition. You also had to care for his horses and break in young ones. At night you might have to sleep at the door of the knight's bedroom.

C The squire did not just learn how to fight and serve his master. Geoffrey Chaucer (1345–1400) wrote this about the squire in his Prologue to the *Canterbury Tales*:
> He knew the way to sit a horse and ride.
> He could make songs and poems and recite,
> Knew how to joust and dance, to draw and write.

By the time you reached the age of 21, you would be ready to become a knight. The quickest way was to be created a knight on the field of battle. This sometimes happened if you had fought well. Otherwise you had to go through a long ceremony.

First you had to be prepared. It began with the cutting of a lock of hair to show your devotion to God. Next you had a bath as a sign that your body was cleansed of sin.

After the bath you were placed on a bed to represent the rest in heaven when you die. Then you were dressed in a white tunic to show that you were pure in mind and body. Over this a red robe was placed to represent the blood you were prepared to shed in the service of God.

On top of all this you put on a black garment as a reminder of the death which one day all men must face.

During the night which followed the first part of the ceremony you had to keep a lonely vigil in front of the altar of a church or chapel. Here you had to remain standing or kneeling for ten hours.

D This drawing by Matthew Paris shows the making of a knight (13th century).

The next morning you would attend a church service. During the service your sword would be blessed. Then you would take the vows of chivalry. These were:
- To fear God and to defend the Christian religion.
- To serve the king faithfully and bravely.
- To protect the weak and defenceless.
- To avoid annoying anybody.
- To live for honour and glory and not money.
- To fight for the good of all.
- To obey those in authority.
- To guard the honour of the knightly order.
- To avoid unfairness, meanness and lies.
- To keep faith and tell the truth.
- To respect women.
- To refuse no challenge from an equal, and never to turn your back on an enemy.

When you left the church you would go in procession to the place where you would be given your armour and sword.

E Jean of Tours described what happened when Geoffrey of Anjou became a knight in 1128:

A Spanish horse of wonderful beauty was provided for Geoffrey, swifter than the flight of birds. He was then armed with a tunic of double-woven mail which no lance or javelin could pierce, and shod with iron boots of the same double mesh. He put on golden spurs. A shield with gold lions was hung around his neck.

A helmet was placed on his head gleaming with many precious stones, and which no sword could pierce or damage. A spear of ash tipped with iron was provided. Finally, from the royal store was brought an ancient sword.

F A 14th-century picture showing three young men being given the sword of knighthood. The figure in brown is a priest.

1. a) What are the boys in source A using instead of a horse?
   b) What other differences can you see?
2. a) Which of the vows of chivalry meant that a knight had to be good at fighting?
   b) Which of the vows meant that a knight had to be kind and honest?
   c) Which of the vows would you find the most difficult to keep? Explain why?
   d) Do you think the vows of chivalry give a realistic idea of what knights were like? Explain your answer.
3. How can you tell from source F that becoming a knight was partly a religious ceremony?

A The Krak des Chevaliers – the most famous of the crusaders' castles.

CHIVALRY – FACT OR FICTION?

The Krak des Chevaliers was one of the biggest and strongest castles to be built in the middle ages. It belonged to the crusaders. These were knights who devoted much of their lives to capturing Jerusalem and the Holy Land from the Turks.

They believed they were doing the work of God. This belief was encouraged by people like St Bernard of Clairvaux. Although he was a monk he believed in fighting for his religion.

B In 1128 he told Christian soldiers that:
> It is not without reason that the soldier of Christ carries a sword; it is for the punishment of the wicked and for the glory of the good.

The crusaders tried to show that they were soldiers of Christ by following a particular way of life. This way of life was called *chivalry* from *chevalier*, the French word for a knight.

Some knights formed themselves into orders like those of the monks. The three main military orders were the Knights Templars, the Knights Hospitallers and the Teutonic Knights. Like the monks, the knights took the vows of poverty, chastity and obedience.

C This was St Bernard's idea of what a crusading knight should be like:
> They cut their hair short, never adorn, seldom wash themselves; they pride themselves on neglected hair, soiled with dust and burnt by the sun and the hauberk. It is wonderful and strange to see them at once as gentle as lambs and as bold as lions. I hardly know whether to call them monks or knights.

D According to others the true story was very different. A writer called John of Salisbury, who also lived in the 12th century, wrote this about chivalry:

> Some think that military glory consists in this, that they shine in elegant dress. Each is boldest in the banqueting hall, but in the battle everyone wants to do least. They have the first places at supper, they feast every day splendidly, if they can afford it. But they avoid work and exercise like a dog or snake.

When Prince Louis of France and rebel barons were defeated at Lincoln, the victorious soldiers were more interested in getting rich than anything else.

E Roger of Wendover in his chronicle *Flowers of History* described what happened:

> The whole city was plundered to the last farthing. Then they proceeded to rob all the churches throughout the city, breaking open all the chests and cupboards with hatchets and hammers. [They seized] gold and silver, cloth of all colours, women's jewellery, gold rings, goblets and precious stones.

F A town being plundered by soldiers in the 14th century.

Two people, living at the same time, could have very different opinions on things that were happening during their lifetime.

1. a) What things are different in sources C and D?
   b) Which vow were the knights breaking in source E?
   c) Suggest reasons why the sources differ.
   d) Should a historian writing about chivalry just choose one source and leave out the others? Give reasons for your answer.
2. Using the sources for information, write your own idea of what chivalry really was.

The military orders were forced to leave the Holy Land in 1219 when they were defeated by the Turks. They left behind some magnificent castles which still stand today.

In England the best time for chivalry was in the 14th century. The most famous order of chivalry at this time was the Order of the Garter. It was founded by Edward III in 1344.

G King Edward III. Notice he is wearing the badge of the garter.

H Froissart (1334–1400) wrote about the Order of the Garter in *Chronicles of England, France, Spain, etc.*

> In the year 1334 there came into the mind of King Edward of England that he would re-build the great castle of Windsor. This is where the noble 'Round Table' was first established. He would make an order of knights and of the bravest youths of his land.

The original membership was limited to the king and 25 other knights. Its emblem was a blue garter bearing the motto *Honi soit qui mal y pense*, which means 'Shame to him who evil thinks'. There are still knights of the garter today – and their motto has not changed.

14 HERALDRY

A The heraldic patterns made it possible to identify knights.

If you went to a football match in which both teams looked the same you would probably find the game difficult to follow. The players would also find it difficult. They would not be able to tell who was on their side.

From the 14th century knights fought battles wearing suits of armour. Even their faces were covered. Imagine the problem of recognising who was on your side. They solved the problem by inventing heraldry. These were colourful designs painted onto their shields.

These designs varied. Often they were simply different patterns painted on the shield. Sometimes they were animals such as lions and eagles.

Each knight had his own personal design. This meant you could tell instantly who was who on the battlefield. This design, called arms, belonged to him alone. No one else was allowed to use a design belonging to another knight.

Officials called heralds had the job of making sure that everybody obeyed this rule.

The heralds gave every part of the shield a name. This made it easy for them to describe it. They always started with the main colour. This was called the field. Then they described how it was divided and what was on the divisions.

The heralds decided who had the right to wear arms and what signs each knight could put on them. Some designs were so popular that there were quarrels over them. The heralds had to settle the arguments. Sometimes, they took away a knight's right to wear arms. They did this if the knight had committed a serious crime.

The heralds carried messages and gave signals in battle. They also counted the dead afterwards. So, they had to know who everyone was.

They organised pageants and mock battles for the pleasure of kings and other important persons. At these tournaments the different contestants could be recognised by their heraldic designs. These were displayed on the shield and on a coat worn over the armour. They were called a coat of arms.

A knight could pass his coat of arms on to his son. The son might want to add more signs. He might want to show who his mother was by

50

adding something from her family's arms. So, as they were passed down, the arms became more complicated.

It was possible to tell a lot from the knight's coat of arms. For instance it might tell you which families he was related to. When a knight married he had the right to add to his own coat of arms those of his wife's family. This was because a woman's property passed on to her husband when she married.

A good example of this is the coat of arms of Richard Neville, the Earl of Warwick. This great nobleman's wealth and power were founded on several fortunate family marriages. He was the most important baron of the time. He died in battle in 1461.

B The family tree shows how Richard Neville inherited from the Montacutes and from the Beauchamps to become both Earl of Salisbury and Earl of Warwick.

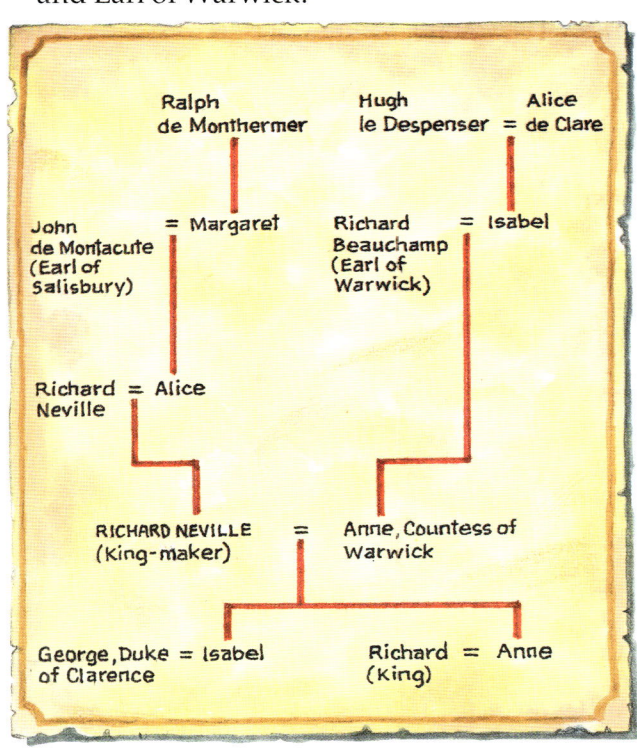

The arms of the Earl of Warwick are made up of seven different designs. Each of these designs comes from one of the families that he was related to.

These are the seven families with a description of their arms:
(i) Beauchamp – red with six yellow crosses
(ii) Montacute – white with three red diamonds
(iii) Monthermer – yellow with a green eagle
(iv) Warwick – blue and yellow chequered with an ermine chevron
(v) Neville – red with a diagonal white cross
(vi) Clare – yellow with three red chevrons
(vii) Despenser – white, red and yellow with a black diagonal line

C The arms of the Earl of Warwick.

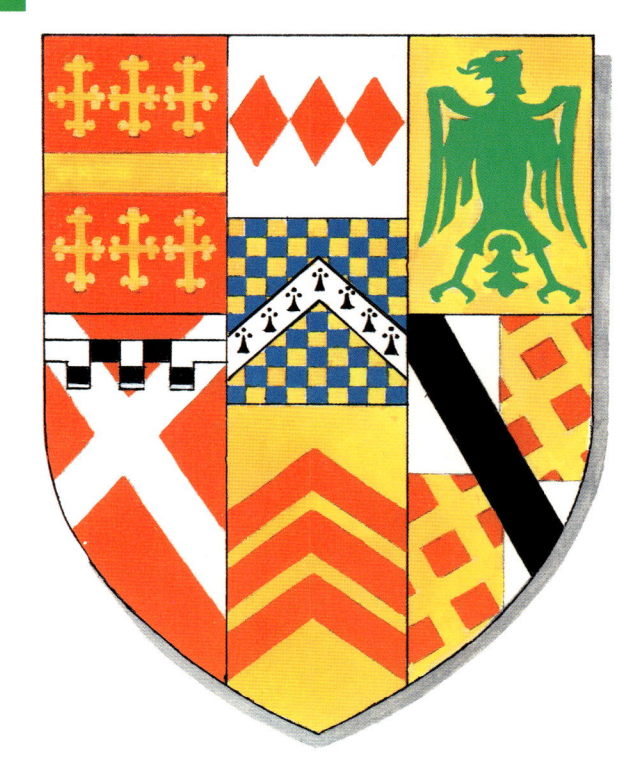

1. a) Write out the family tree of the Earl of Warwick.
   b) Next to each family name, draw and colour the shield belonging to that family.
   c) Which coats of arms did Richard Neville inherit from his wife Anne?
2. Look at source A. Apart from on shields, where else was the knight's coat of arms displayed?
3. Describe each of the eight different designs on source A.
4. Why do you think designs such as lions and eagles were favourite animals to have on shields?
5. Source A is from a book of heraldry listing the names of knights with a picture of their coat of arms. Why would such a book need to be kept by the heralds?
6. Today there are many different designs that tell us who something belongs to.
   a) Draw some designs that you know; such as your school's badge, your favourite football team or a company logo.
   b) What is the difference between badges today and heraldry in the middle ages?

15 TOURNAMENTS

The tournament was a military sports meeting. It was a way of training for war. It meant the knights could use their warlike energies in times of peace.

The early tournaments were more like real battles than a sport. The contestants used real weapons and it was quite common for people to get killed. Gradually, as it became more popular, tournaments grew into a spectator sport. They were followed by thousands of keen fans. There were strict rules enforced by referees and officials. Edward I set up a Court of Chivalry to settle arguments which often happened during tournaments.

A In 1292 he laid down rules in what was called *The Statute of Arms.* Here are some of the rules:

i) **No knight to have more than three squires in arms to help him at the tournament.**

iii) No knight or squire attending the tournament is to carry a pointed sword or dagger, but only a broad sword for the tourney.

viii) Those who come to watch the tournament must not be armed with any manner of armour, and must not carry any sword, dagger, stick or stone.

There were two types of contest at a tournament. The tourney was a fight with swords between a large number of knights in two teams. Not surprisingly things often used to get out of hand. There were a lot of casualties – even deaths – during a tourney.

The other type of contest was the joust. This was an encounter between two mounted knights. Each was usually armed with a lance. It was fitted with a small metal crown on the pointed end. This was to soften the blow and prevent serious injury.

B The joust, a scene from a 15th-century manuscript.

In the joust the object was to knock your opponent off his horse. Each pair of knights charged at each other until one of them fell to the ground. During the 14th century a fence known as a tilt was put up to prevent the two horses colliding.

The joust opened with the opposing knights taking up their positions at either end of the lists. At this moment they held their lances at rest. When the starter gave the command they raised their lances. They gripped them loosely so that the shock of impact would not be likely to break their wrists. Lowering the points of their weapons leftwards to an angle of 45 degrees to the horse's neck, they charged down the lists.

The shock of the heavily-armed men and horses meeting at full tilt sometimes knocked them both off. If not, they would turn and charge again in the opposite direction. When one contender was unhorsed, the other got off and the contest continued on foot with swords.

C The importance of tournaments as a training for war is mentioned by Roger de Hoveden in his Chronicle written in the 12th century:
A youth must have seen his blood flow and felt his teeth crack under the blow of his adversary, and have been thrown to the ground twenty times. Only then will he be able to face real war with the hope of victory.

Tournaments usually lasted for three or four days. Two were devoted to jousting and one to the tourney. The evenings were given over to feasting, music and dancing. The fourth day might have sports such as archery and wrestling.

D An illustration from a 14th-century manuscript.

The contests caused a lot of excitement and they attracted a large crowd of spectators. The most enthusiastic onlookers were the fashionable ladies who watched the proceedings from a specially built grandstand.

E In 1348 Henry Knighton, the Leicester chronicler, commented on these ladies.
They dressed in men's clothes in coloured tunics, one colour or pattern on the right side and another on the left. With short hoods that had pendants like ropes round their necks, and belts thickly studded with gold or silver, a gang of women would come to share the sport. Sometimes there were forty or fifty ladies, of the fairest and prettiest (though I say not of the best) among the whole kingdom.

F This is a 15th-century illustration.

1 a) Look at sources D and F. Which is a real battle and which is a tournament?
  b) Give as many reasons as you can for your answer.
2 a) Look at source B. Who are the men on horseback on the far right and left of the picture?
  b) Which extract refers to these men?
3 a) Which source gives a reason why tournaments were held?
  b) What is the reason?
4 a) Why do you think Edward I made the rules in source A?
  b) What did the writer of source E think of the ladies who went to tournaments?

A lot of history is about change. At the same time some things do not change. We call this continuity.

5 a) How did tournaments change?
  b) What things stayed the same?

16 THE END OF THE MONASTERIES

By the 16th century, the monasteries were under attack. People said that the monks and nuns were lazy. They said that they were not keeping to their vows. Some people even thought that monasteries were out of date and should be got rid of.

However, not everybody felt like this. Plenty of people could think of good reasons for keeping monasteries. For a start they were a great help to travellers.

A A report on monasteries in 1535 had this to say about the abbey of Netley:
> Being a large building situated near the coast, it is a great relief and comfort to the king's subjects and strangers travelling on the sea.

Another thing that people liked was the way monasteries looked after the poor. If you were starving you could depend on the monks and nuns. They would never turn you away without giving you food. It was also normal for monks to give clothes to those begging at the gate of the monastery.

B The report of 1535 said this about Catesby nunnery:
> The nuns do much to the relief of the king's people, and his grace's poor subjects are also much helped.

C Some monasteries went even further than this. A 16th-century writer called John Leland wrote this about the abbot of Glastonbury:
> He made an almshouse in the northern part of the abbey for seven or ten poor women with a chapel.

There were other things that the monasteries did for ordinary people. In many towns they provided the only health care available. In some places the monks gave lessons to boys. Girls might learn how to read and write in nunneries.

The good things that monasteries did were not enough to stop them being attacked. This did not matter too much if ordinary people complained about them. It was a different matter if the king turned against them – especially if the king was Henry VIII.

Between 1536 and 1540 every monastery in England and Wales was closed on the orders of the king. In some parts of the country people tried to stop this happening. In the north a great army of rebels gathered. They were led by a man called Robert Aske. They wanted to march to London and try to force Henry to change his mind.

The rebels were stopped well before they reached London. They were persuaded to surrender when they were told that nobody would be punished. However, as soon as the rebel army had broken up and gone home the leaders were arrested.

D Before Robert Aske suffered the terrible death of a traitor, he wrote down the reasons why he had rebelled.
> The abbeys in the north gave great help to poor men and served God well. The abbeys were one of the beauties of this country to all men and strangers passing through the land. Also all gentlemen were given help with money. Their young sons were looked after. In nunneries their daughters were brought up to be kind and gentle.
>
> Those abbeys which were near the coast were great builders of sea walls and ditches. They built bridges and highways and other such things for the common good.

E This is how one 19th-century artist imagined the end of the monasteries.

Henry had several reasons for wanting to get rid of the monasteries. Probably the most important was that he wanted to get his hands on their great wealth.

F When Henry replied to the demands of the rebels, however, he did not mention this:

> No monastery was closed down where God was well served. This only happened to those where there was mischief and evil living. And as for their hospitality, for the relief of poor people, we wonder you are not ashamed to say that they have been a great help to our people. A great many, or most of them, have no more than four or five religious people in them. Several had only one.

Sometimes accounts of the past can be very different. Sometimes they have more to do with a person's opinion than with the truth. When this happens we say that a person has a biased point of view.

G This 16th-century painting shows Henry VIII on his deathbed passing on his kingdom to his son Edward VI in 1547.

1 a) What are the two main reasons Henry gives for closing the monasteries?
   b) Why did Henry not mention the real reason why he wanted to close them?
   c) Is there anything in source F which shows that Henry VIII was not telling the truth? Explain your answer.
   d) Why is source D likely to be just as biased as source F?

2 a) What view does source E give about the end of the monasteries?
   b) How does the artist put over this view?
   c) Is the treasure on view a comment on the monks or Henry? Explain your answer.

3 a) Who are the people in source G, other than Henry VIII and Edward VI?
   b) How does the way the artist has painted these people show that he supported Henry?

4 Is source G more likely to be true because it is a primary source?

5 Using all the sources, write a balanced view of monasteries before Henry VIII got rid of them.

17 THE END OF CASTLES

During the 15th and 16th centuries castles gradually became less popular with rich people. Barons were abandoning their castles and letting them fall into ruins. This was a gradual change and continued over a long period. There were several reasons why castles came to an end:
- War had become more about battles between armies than besieging castles.
- The end of the Wars of the Roses in 1485 led to more peaceful times.
- Cannons became powerful enough to smash down castles.
- Government was based more in London than before. This meant that the king no longer had to travel around so much. So he needed fewer castles to stay at.
- Castles were too uncomfortable. Barons expected a higher standard of living than was possible in most castles.

Not all causes are the same. Some are short term and others are long term. The short-term causes take effect fairly quickly. Long-term causes take a longer time to bring about change.

1 a) Of the five causes listed above, which one is a short-term cause?
   b) For each of the others, explain why they are long-term causes.

Barons did not suddenly stop building castles. For a long time castles continued to be a status symbol. You could always say you were an important person if you owned a castle. But slowly things did start to change. Barons became concerned about making their castles comfortable to live in. It was no longer so important to have strong fortifications.

In some places barons built castles that were more like manor houses. An early example was Stokesay Castle. It was bought by Laurence of Ludlow in 1280. At this time it had a moat and a small stone tower. To these he added a luxurious house, with a private room and a great hall with huge windows.

Laurence had to make sure he could defend his house because Stokesay was near the Welsh border. In 1291 he obtained a licence from the king to crenellate his mansion. He surrounded its courtyard with a high wall.

He built a new tower some 20 metres high. Its main purpose was to serve as a place of safety in an emergency. It could not be entered from any other part of the building. You could only get into it by a ladder from the courtyard to a door in the wall 2 metres above ground level.

A Stokesay Castle has changed very little since the time when Laurence of Ludlow built it. The great hall is shown to the right of the tower.

The invention of cannons took much longer to bring about the end of castles. Cannons began to appear early in the 14th century. For a long time they were not much good for attacking castles. There were several reasons for this:
- Early guns were not made in one piece. They were made of iron bars welded together and bound with iron hoops like a barrel. As a result they were not very strong.
- Gunpowder was at first weak and made it hard for gunners to judge how much to use.
- They were slow to fire which meant that there were long pauses between shots.
- It was difficult to move the heavy cannons from one place to another. They were often a long way behind the rest of the army.

B A siege using cannon from a picture in a 15th-century manuscript.

Cannons were more useful for the defenders of a castle. They were able to fix them in prepared and safe positions. Their range was short so they were used to cover the ground immediately in front of the walls. The defenders of the castle fired them through gunports shaped like an upside-down keyhole. There was a round hole for the gun to fire through. Above this there was a slit for the gunner to aim the gun at the target.

2 What made the great hall at Stokesay Castle (source A) a dangerous place to be during an attack?
3 a) How are cannons being used in source B?
   b) What other methods are being used to attack the castle?
   c) How effective would the cannons be, compared with the other methods?

C Bodiam Castle was one of the first castles specially designed to use cannons. They could stop the enemy from coming too near by firing through keyhole ports like this one.

57

18 FIELDWORK – CASTLES

Many cathedrals and castles, as well as abbeys and priories, are still standing. Some, like Windsor Castle, are complete. Others look just like a pile of stones. Some buildings, like Salisbury Cathedral, continue to be used for their original purpose. Others are totally deserted. Most of these places can be visited and we can learn a lot from what remains today.

When you look at an old building you have to bear several things in mind. First, there may be a lot missing that was once part of the building. For instance, a lot of ruined castles have got floors and roofs missing. In general, only hard-wearing materials like stone survive.

It is also likely that the building has been added to at various stages in its lifetime. You can see this easily if an extension has been built in a different material or a different size of stones.

It is often possible to see several layers showing changes made in earlier times. This can happen if a window or doorway had been filled in. Also old windows may have gone out of fashion and new ones added instead.

Sometimes it is possible to use written sources to help us understand the remains. To find out what happened in source A, we have the work of a monk from Barnwell Abbey to help us.

B *The Barnwell Chronicle* records the siege of Rochester Castle in 1215:
> King John gave orders for blacksmiths to make many iron picks. He put expert miners to work. They cut their way underground until at last they were under one of the great corner towers.
> After two months when the miners came out, brushwood and branches were carried into the tunnel and fat from forty pigs. Then a fire was started. All the timbers caught fire and blazed until they collapsed. With a great roar the whole roof gave way and the tower fell down.

After reading this, change your answer to question 1b), if necessary. Source C will also help you.

A One corner of the keep of Rochester Castle.

1 a) What do you notice looks strange about the wall in source A?
b) Why do you think it was built this way?

C The outside of the keep of Rochester Castle.

Features like those in sources A and C will tell you a lot about the way the castle was built. To understand life in the castle you need to put yourself in the place of the people who lived there.

For instance, you could imagine the year is 1139. King Stephen is besieging Ludlow castle. You are employed as a spy by the king and you have managed to get into the castle. You have been sent to examine the outside and the inside of the inner bailey defences. You must report back to the king:
- The nature of the defences.
- Your advice on how to attack.
- The best way to approach the castle without being seen.

Another possibility is to go back to the year 1483. You are the 12-year-old Edward, Prince of Wales, living in Ludlow Castle with your brother. The news arrives of the death of your father, King Edward IV, and plans are made for you to travel to London to be crowned as the new king.

But late one night, a nobleman comes to see you secretly in your room in the Pendover Tower. He tells of rumours that your uncle Richard has made plans to stop this happening. You decide to escape!

In this case you would have to plan how to escape from the castle without being seen.

When visiting a castle it is a good idea to have a check-list of questions. These questions will help you to know what to look for in a castle:

- Is there a ditch around the outside of the castle?
- Is it wet or dry?
- How wide is it?
- Which is the easiest side to approach if you were attacking the castle?
- How high are the walls?
- On which side are there most towers?
- Are they round or square or a mixture?
- Does the castle have a keep?
- Which walls are overlooked by the keep?
- Are the towers thicker at their bases?
- Where are the openings for letting off arrows?
- Where are the gateways?
- Do they have portcullises or drawbridges?
- What is missing from the castle compared with when it was new?

> **2** Use the information on Ludlow Castle on pages 12–13 and answer as many questions as possible from the check-list.

Another activity which helps you understand the layout of the castle is to design a guide. You need a plan of the castle, such as Caerphilly on page 39. Then choose several positions around the castle. They need to be in places where you can see important parts of the castle. You mark these on the plan. When you have chosen the positions on the plan, you can write a description of what you can see at each point.

> **3** a) Draw a plan of Caerphilly Castle (page 39).
> b) Choose six positions. They should be spread around the castle.
> c) Write a brief description of what you could see at each position. Use the points of the compass to give instructions about which direction to look.

D Some castles are still in use today. Leeds Castle, seen here, is sometimes used for meetings between heads of government because it is easy to guard.

19 FIELDWORK-CATHEDRALS AND MONASTERIES

A A visit to Much Wenlock Priory in Shropshire.

Most of our medieval cathedrals are still standing and are still used for services. You might think that this makes it fairly easy to work out their history. Perhaps – if the cathedral was built as a complete design with few later changes.

The problem is that most cathedrals were built over many years with lots of changes and extensions. With monasteries, it is even more difficult. Most of them are in ruins. A lot of guesswork is needed to understand what they once looked like. However, there are some clues to help us understand these buildings.

The first thing is to find out the layout of the separate parts of the monastery. Plans of most of them are available. The biggest buildings such as the church are usually quite easy to spot.

When you have worked out the layout you can start to look at the buildings in more detail. This will give you clues to the building methods used. You can find out what type of stone was used. You can also look at the different uses for arches. You will often find these come in many shapes and sizes.

In many cases the arches are decorated with elaborate carvings. You may come across other examples of decoration. Sometimes the stone capitals at the base of the arches provide evidence of the work of the medieval stone masons. In some monasteries there are floor tiles decorated with various designs.

In the case of cathedrals you have to decide what has been added since the 16th century. You will usually discover that some of the windows and many of the fittings inside have been added. However, in most cases, many medieval features remain.

Many cathedrals have the tombs of kings, barons and bishops. These tombs are usually highly decorated. They often feature a life-size figure of the person buried in the cathedral.

Winchester Cathedral contains the tomb of William of Wykeham. He was the Bishop of Winchester from 1366–1404. The tomb was planned during his lifetime and was ready when he was buried on 27 September 1404. Although he died at the age of 80, the effigy shows him in middle age. The tomb was put on the place where, as a boy, he had stood to listen to the services.

The tomb is placed in a part of the cathedral called a chantry chapel. Chantry comes from the French word *chanter* to sing. In this chapel prayers were said for William. Special services were held every year on the anniversary of his death.

The tombs of saints were once an important part of a cathedral. However, most of these were removed when Henry VIII closed the monasteries.

B The figure of William of Wykeham still has some of its original paint.

C Denny Abbey, in Cambridgeshire, showing evidence of a number of alterations in the stonework.

Using an old building as a historical source is rather like a detective looking for clues. If you know what clues to look for you can build up a picture of what it was like in the middle ages.

It is possible to trace the history of the buildings from what is left. Any alterations usually leave their mark. This could be in the form of windows or doorways filled in. There may be steps that lead nowhere. Sometimes there are marks left on a wall where there was once a roof. Holes in the wall are caused for various reasons. They are often the places where the beams for the floor slotted into the wall. Or they may be put-log holes. These are the holes for scaffolding used by the builders.

It is often easy to see how a stream was diverted so as to supply the kitchen and flush the rere-dorter. The monks were ahead of their time when it came to the supply of water. A lot of monasteries still have the remains of the channels that took water to different parts of the site.

D An outline sketch of Denny Abbey.

1. Draw an outline sketch of Denny Abbey, like the one in source D, and mark on it the following features:
   (a) remains of pillars,
   (b) patching of wall,
   (c) blocked window,
   (d) new windows and
   (e) blocked doorway.

2. a) Why do you think William of Wykeham decided to have source B made for himself?
   b) Why did it show him as he looked some years before he died?

3. What information can you learn from looking at source B?

4. Plan a visit to a ruined monastery like Castle Acre Priory (pages 32–33). Make a checklist of things to look for.

61

20 CHANGE AND CONTINUITY

A The great hall of Castle Hedingham in Essex built around 1140.

The Black Death of 1348–50 may have killed almost one third of the population. Many knights died, so their numbers were reduced. Long periods of warfare such as the Hundred Years War, 1337–1453, also added to their decline. Some people who were expected to give knight service paid money instead. This further reduced the number of knights.

It caused problems for the barons. Their duty was to supply the king with knights. They found it more and more necessary to hire mercenaries. These were soldiers who would fight in return for money. They were always ready to change masters if they were offered more pay. When they were paid to guard a castle, the baron could not be sure that they would stay with him. They might even turn on him.

For safety's sake it was best not to mix too freely with the mercenaries. The barons decided to keep their living quarters separate from those of the family. In some of the later castles the baron lived in the gatehouse. If the mercenaries became threatening he could control the entrance.

Another major development was the change in the use of the great hall. At one time this was the centre of all life in the castle. It was used by both the baron and his family as well as the servants. Over the years it became more and more common for the baron and his family to live in private rooms. Another change was the greater emphasis on comfort. Most barons expected a higher standard of living than in earlier years.

An example of this was Bodiam Castle. It was built by Sir Edward Dalyngrigge in 1385. He was given a licence to build himself a fortification 'in defence of the country against the king's enemies'. This was because Bodiam was in the danger area of French raids on the Kent and Sussex coast.

Dalyngrigge himself had good reason to fear the French. He had rampaged through France as a bandit rather than a soldier. Returning with enough money to build a castle, he married an heiress. Her property included the land at Bodiam.

The castle has two quite separate sets of rooms. One lot was for the baron, the other for his servants. From the outside it looks just like a normal castle. However, on the inside it is more like a comfortable manor house.

B Tattershall Castle – castle or house?

C Bodiam Castle in Sussex looks like a typical castle on the outside.

Some so-called castles were even less like the normal type. Tattershall Castle, built in 1443, is really a private house built to look like a castle. The windows were far too large for defence. It was made from about 300,000 red bricks especially imported from abroad. No expense was spared to make the rooms as luxurious as possible.

So, by 1500, castles had changed a lot since the time of the Normans. Despite all these changes barons and other rich people still wanted to have a house that looked like a castle. This is an example of what we call continuity. It is the opposite of change. You have continuity when things stay the same. In this case, the castles had changed, but people continued to want the same thing.

In fact, people continued to build castles for the next 400 years. In most cases these people did not need castles to defend themselves. They thought that their houses would be more impressive if they looked like a castle.

If we compare castles with our houses today we can see even more changes and less continuity. Source A has one or two examples of continuity. Most things, however, are quite different from what you would find in a modern house.

1. List the changes in the design of castles during the middle ages. You can add to your list from earlier chapters.
2. a) What parts of source B are like normal castles?
   b) Why did rich people continue to build castles even though, like source B, they were useless for war?
3. a) List as many differences as you can between source A and a room today.
   b) Which features are similar?

GLOSSARY

adorn – wear fine clothes
adversary – opponent
alms – gifts of money, food or clothing for the poor
almshouse – house for poor people
ancestor – dead relative from earlier generation
capital – top part of a pillar or column
carrel – small cubicle
cartulary – collection of documents
cesspit – pit for collecting sewage
chamberlain – official in a monastery who looked after the monks' clothes
chancel – eastern end of a church containing the high altar
chaplain – person performing the duties of a priest
chevron – shape made by two diagonal lines
chronicle – history of events
Cinque Ports – certain ports on the coast of south-east England
convent – group of monks or nuns
counter-attack – attack on an enemy who has already attacked you
crenellate – put up fortifications
crozier – staff shaped like a shepherd's crook
dean – head of a cathedral
decapitated – having your head cut off
diocese – area ruled by a bishop
effigy – copy of a person's body
ermine – white fur with black markings
farthing – one quarter of an old penny
fortification – part of a building designed to protect it from attack
garrison – soldiers in a castle
garth – yard
Gothic – styles of architecture in the 12th-16th centuries
hauberk – coat of armour made from rings joined together called mail
heir – person who receives property on the death of a close relative
hurdle – moveable fence
infirmary – hospital
joust – combat between two men on horseback

leeches – bloodsucking worm
lists – wooden railings around the area in which a tournament was held
machicolation – openings in the floor of a projecting platform along the top of a castle wall
manuscript – book or paper written by hand
masonry – part of a building made of stone
minstrel – musician
multure – right to mill corn
naval supremacy – overall control of the sea
nave – central part of a church
novice – person learning to be a monk or nun
ordinance – order or rule
pageant – colourful procession
palisade – wall made of strong wooden stakes
parapet – wall protecting soldiers from attack
parboiled – partly boiled
pilgrim – visitor to a holy place
plundered – stealing property during a raid
portcullis – wooden or iron grating dropped into a gateway to prevent people entering a castle
prior – abbot's deputy in an abbey or head of a priory
recite – read out aloud
shrine – holy place
siesta – midday nap
stall – seating in a church
status symbol – sign of wealth or power
tenant – person renting land
terrain – landscape
tilting – charging with a lance at an opponent
tourney – contest between two teams of armed men
transept – extensions to the side aisles of a cathedral crossing at right angles to the rest of the church
treachery – act of betrayal
veil – piece of material covering the face
vigil – the ordeal of keeping awake and praying throughout the night
vow – a solemn promise